T0208987

Words That Heal THE Blues

Other Inspirational Books by Douglas Bloch

Words That Heal: Affirmations and Meditations for Daily Living

*Listening to Your Inner Voice: Discover the Truth Within You
and Let It Guide Your Way*

*I Am With You Always: A Treasury of Inspirational Quotations,
Poems, and Prayers*

The Power of Positive Talk: Words to Help Every Child Succeed

Healing from Depression: 12 Weeks to a Better Mood

Words That Heal the Blues

AFFIRMATIONS & MEDITATIONS FOR LIVING OPTIMALLY WITH MOOD DISORDERS

A Daily Mental Health Recovery Program

DOUGLAS BLOCH, M.A.

CELESTIAL ARTS

Berkeley

All rights reserved. Published in the United States by Celestial Arts, an imprint
of the Crown Publishing Group, a division of Random House, Inc., New York.
www.crownpublishing.com
www.tenspeed.com

Celestial Arts and the Celestial Arts colophon are registered trademarks of
Random House, Inc.

Library of Congress Cataloging-in-Publication Data

Bloch, Douglas, 1949–
  Words that heal the blues : affirmations & meditations for living optimally with
mood disorders : a daily mental health recovery program / Douglas Bloch.
      p. cm.
 1. Affective disorders. 2. Affective disorders—Treatment. 3. Affirmations.
I. Title.
RC537.B5355 2004
616.85'27—dc22
                              2003022476

ISBN 978-1-58761-198-8

Cover design by Catherine Jacobes
Interior design by Chloe Rawlins

First Edition

                 145052501

Blessed are those who confess their pain and brokenness,
for they shall take hold of their healing.
Blessed are those who wrestle with their own darkness,
for they shall touch again the light from which they came.

    —Rodney Romney, *Wilderness Spirituality*

Dedication

To all who feel or have felt helpless in the face of mental illness. May they feel empowered to help themselves, and may they know they are not alone.

Contents

Acknowledgments

❧

I would like to begin by thanking Jo Ann Deck and the staff at Celestial Arts for their support in bringing vital information about the treatment of depression to the general public. That support began with the publication of *Healing from Depression: 12 Weeks to a Better Mood* in 2002 and continues with the publishing of this work, *Words That Heal the Blues*.

My first collection of affirmations, *Words That Heal*, which was originally published in 1988, inspired *Words That Heal the Blues*. I would like to thank its readers for making the book a well-loved classic on affirmations.

I also want to thank the brave and courageous souls who attended my anxiety and depression support groups over the past three years. The healing they experienced is testimony to the effectiveness of the holistic treatment for depression that I outline in *Healing from Depression* and *Words That Heal the Blues*.

I also express appreciation to my partner, Joan, for helping me run these groups.

Finally, I would like to thank my Portland editor, Joan Bridgman. Her comments and suggestions—especially in the formation of the affirmations—helped simplify the book and make it a more potent vehicle for healing and transformation.

Who This Book Is For

☙

50% of all Americans will experience a mental or emotional disorder sometime during their lives.

—The U.S. Surgeon General,
"The State of the Nation's Mental Health," 1999

As with my previous book *Healing from Depression, Words That Heal the Blues* grew out of my personal experience as a depression survivor as well as my clinical work in facilitating depression and anxiety support groups. Although the affirmations and meditations in this book target those who suffer from depressive illnesses, I find that virtually *anyone* who struggles with a mental or emotional disorder can use them. This includes a great many people. According to the surgeon general in the 1999 publication "The State of the Nation's Mental Health," 22 percent of all Americans suffer a mental or emotional disorder in any given year, and *half* of all Americans are afflicted over the course of a lifetime.

In the report the surgeon general defined mental disorders as *"health conditions marked by alterations in thinking, mood or behavior that cause distress or impair a person's ability to function."* These conditions include the following:

- depression
- bipolar disorder
- generalized anxiety disorder

- panic attacks
- PTSD (post-traumatic stress disorder)
- attention deficit disorder
- alcoholism
- drug addiction
- eating disorders
- phobias
- schizophrenia

Moreover, the self-care strategies outlined in the daily lessons can help you deal with the following "situational stressors":

- health problems
- work or financial crises
- grief over the loss of a loved one
- the ending or beginning of relationships
- periods of transition

Thus, whether you suffer from a mental/emotional disorder or face a difficult challenge, the practical coping strategies outlined in this book can make a positive difference in your life. I wish you the best on your healing journey.

Introduction: How to Use This Book

ৎৡৢ

May all sentient beings have happiness and its causes.

May all sentient beings be free from suffering and its causes.

May all sentient beings not be separated from sorrowless bliss.

May all sentient beings abide in equanimity, free from bias, attachment and anger.

—Tibetan Buddhist prayer for the alleviation of suffering

Words That Heal the Blues is a collection of affirmations and meditations designed to help you live optimally, balance your mood, and alleviate the symptoms of anxiety, depression, and other mood disorders. The book is structured around a series of daily lessons, each of which contains the following:

1. A daily meditation
2. A series of affirmations focusing on the day's topic—positive thoughts and ideas
3. A quotation that encapsulates the essence of the day's lesson
4. A self-care activity for the day

The basic way to use this book is to read one lesson a day, so that you cycle through the material approximately once a month, or every thirty days (specific ways to do this are provided on page 27). As you revisit the lessons each month, their meditations and affirmations will become etched into your brain and nervous system, creating new circuits and pathways.

You can also use this book as a source of "mental first aid." If you begin to feel distressed by negative thoughts or feelings, look through the contents and locate a daily lesson that speaks to your condition. Read over the lesson, using it as a source of comfort, guidance, and support. You may also turn to a daily lesson simply because you are inspired to do so. No specific formula exists for using this book. Let yourself be guided to the words that touch your heart.

In addition, feel free to share the material in this book with friends or family members who might seek comfort or inspiration. *Anyone* who seeks to bring greater wellness and harmony into his or her life can use the affirmations and meditations.

Finally, I include additional resources in the book's appendices.

Appendix A provides an overview of the signs and symptoms of a number of mood disorders, including clinical depression, bipolar disorder, generalized anxiety disorder, and panic disorder.

Appendix B contains a series of sample affirmations that occur under six distinct headings: self-esteem, love and relationships, health, work/vocation, prosperity, and spiritual development.

Appendix C explains how to create a vision statement of wellness in a clear and precise picture of mental and emotional well-being.

As you work with this material, remember that progress toward health is not a straight line. Temporary setbacks sometimes interrupt periods of forward movement. Take heart that progress will continue. If you set the intention to heal, reach out for support, and apply the self-care strategies outlined in this book, you will experience positive results. Best wishes on your transformational journey.

The Three Pillars
of Mental Health Recovery

In my work facilitating mental health recovery groups, I discovered that the recovery process consists of three life-changing steps.

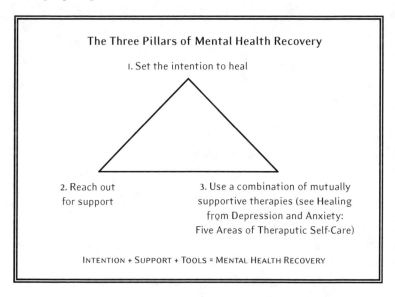

The Three Pillars of Mental Health Recovery

1. Set the intention to heal

2. Reach out for support

3. Use a combination of mutually supportive therapies (see Healing from Depression and Anxiety: Five Areas of Theraputic Self-Care)

INTENTION + SUPPORT + TOOLS = MENTAL HEALTH RECOVERY

Step 1: Set the intention to heal. Make the decision that you want to get well, even if you don't know how. Setting the intention to heal is the starting point of all recovery. Lesson 1 specifically addresses this principle.

Step 2: Reach out for support. Love and connection are essential parts of the healing process. When you share the power of intention with others, it is magnified. When we state our vision of wellness in the presence of one or more supportive people, that vision becomes strengthened and exponentially magnified.

Step 3: Treat your symptoms using a combination of mutually supportive therapies. You can see an example of this integrative approach in the way doctors treat heart disease. If you ask a cardiologist how to prevent a heart attack (or to recover from one), he or she might prescribe a cholesterol-lowering medication and tell you to eat a low-fat diet, exercise three to four times a week, and cut down on the stress in your life.

In a similar manner, you can holistically treat depression and other mood disorders on a variety of levels. In working to achieve my own emotional balance, I identified five such levels—physical self-care, mental/emotional self-care, social support, spiritual connection, and lifestyle habits. (The diagram on the opposite page depicts a visual overview of these areas.) You will learn about the self-care strategies listed in the diagram in lessons 2 through 31.

In working with hundreds of people who suffer from mood disorders, I consistently find that when people take these three steps, they invariably begin to feel better and experience a reduction of their symptoms.

Now, let's turn our attention to one of my favorite tools of self-healing—the affirmation.

Healing from Depression and Anxiety:
Five Areas of Therapeutic Self-Care*

THE GOAL: TO EXPERIENCE A BETTER MOOD, FREE FROM DEPRESSION AND ANXIETY.

Activities that support my vision of wellness

Physical self-care
Exercise
Nutrition
Water intake
Hydrotherapy
Natural light
Sleep
Medication
Supplements
Herbs
Acupuncture
Breathing
Yoga
Touch

Spiritual connection
Prayer
Meditation
Spiritual community
Inspirational texts
Forgiveness
The 12 Steps of AA
Finding purpose
    and meaning

Lifestyle habits
Structure/routine
Time in nature
Fulfilling work
Setting goals
Relaxation
Pleasurable activities
Humor
Music therapy
Creative self-expression
Time for beauty
Stress reduction
Time management

Mental and emotional self-care
Restructuring cognitive
    processes
Practicing daily affirmations
Releasing negative beliefs
Taming the inner critic
Charting your moods
Feeling your feelings
Thinking like an optimist
Keeping a gratitude journal
Overcoming the stigma
    of depression
Self-forgiveness
Psychotherapy
Healing family of origin issues
Working through grief

Social support
Family
Friends
Psychiatrist/therapist
Minister/rabbi
Support group
Day treatment
Volunteer work
Pets and animals

* This program is meant to support, not replace,
any medical treatment you may be receiving.

Affirmations:
Their Role in Uplifting Your Mood

༫

Colin flushed triumphantly. He had made himself believe
he was going to get well which was really more than half
the battle if he had been aware of it.

—Frances Hodgson Burnett, *The Secret Garden*

In his classic book *Seven Habits of Highly Effective People*, Stephen Covey states habit number 2: "Begin with the end in mind." Covey says this habit is fundamental because all things are created twice—first in the mind and then in the world of form. A powerful way to apply this principle is by creating an affirmation, which I define as "a *positive thought* or *idea* on which you consciously focus to produce a desired result."

The apostle Paul was probably thinking about affirmations when he wrote, "Whatever things are true, whatever things are lovely, whatever things are of good report, . . . think on these things" (Philippians 4:8). This wisdom has been validated by modern-day neuroscientists whose research demonstrates that every thought produces a chemical reaction in the brain, which in turn corresponds to a feeling. As one brain scientist explained it, *every thought has a neurochemical equivalent* (see the diagram below).

Thought ⟷ chemical reaction ⟷ feeling

Researchers have discovered that people who suffer from anxiety and depression tend to dwell on negative thoughts that produce a low or anxious mood. These thoughts fall into the following areas:

- regrets about the past
- fears about the future
- negative statements and criticisms directed toward ourselves

Affirmations (positive self-statements) are a simple and time-proven way of redirecting the mind to accentuate the positive. They closely follow the principles stated in cognitive behavioral therapy, which is the psychotherapy most often used to treat anxiety and depression. When you write or say an affirmation, you turn your mind to something positive, and the negative has no place to dwell. It's as if the neurons light up a different pathway or circuit in the brain. The repetition of affirmations over time changes negative fear-producing thoughts into positive uplifting ones, thereby leading to a change in mood.

How to Create Healing Affirmations

Using affirmations is a simple and enjoyable process. You can create an affirmation to bring about a specific *goal* or *outcome* (doing well in school, making new friends, or improving one's health) or an improved *attitude* or *state of mind* (experiencing self-love or overcoming fear). You can create an affirmation for virtually any need, goal, or challenge in life. What follows is a method that I find to be quite effective.

Pick an area of your life that needs healing. Most mood disorders affect four areas of experience. These include one's *thinking* (for example, low self-esteem or self-criticism), *feelings* (for example, sad or empty mood, fear), *physical well-being* (for example, sleep problems or eating disturbances), and *behaviors* (for example, a decrease in activity or social withdrawal). Pick an area you want to address.

Decide what you want to occur in that area of your life. Ask yourself, "What outcome am I seeking? What would it look and feel like if this part of my life improved?" For example, if your problem is poor sleep, the desired outcome would be deep and restful sleep. If you suffer from low self-esteem, your goal would be healthy self-esteem.

Formulate the desired outcome as a positive statement. When you say, *"I am not sleeping poorly,"* the subconscious mind screens out the *not* and hears *"I am sleeping poorly."* (Or if someone says, "Don't think of pink elephants," that exact image immediately comes to mind.) To prevent this from occurring, rephrase the affirmation to directly state what you want—for example, *"My sleep is sound and restful."*

Use the present tense, as if the outcome were happening in this moment. Thus, instead of stating *"I will exercise regularly,"* you would say *"I exercise regularly."* Can you feel the difference as you repeat these words to yourself or say them out loud?

Experience how the affirmation feels. Once you write your affirmation, say it to yourself a few times, and tune into how it sounds and feels. When you find a good affirmation, you will feel a sense of rightness in your gut. If the affirmation doesn't quite feel right, fine-tune it by altering one or two words. Thus *"I am experiencing peace"* may work better if stated as *"I am at peace"* or *"I am peaceful."*

Repeat your affirmation each day. Say it to yourself, say it out loud, and write it down. Repetition and consistency are necessary to create new neuronal circuits in the brain. Consider the affirmation "Every day, in every way, I am getting better and better." The French pharmacist Emile Coué popularized this affirmation at the beginning of the twentieth century. Many of Coué's patients reported healings when they repeated this suggestion again and again.

Another example concerns the boxing great Muhammad Ali. When Ali first proclaimed "I am the greatest," he was a relatively unknown boxer named Cassius Clay. Ten years and thousands of repetitions later, the world hailed him as the greatest fighter of all time. Ali's repetition of the good he desired became a self-fulfilling prophecy.

When you repeat an affirmation, you impress its thought pattern on your mind, thereby transforming your previously held mental patterns. The more you use your affirmation, the more rapid and powerful the change will be. Soon its words will become a living presence in your awareness.

Be consistent. It is essential to use your affirmation regularly to benefit from the principle of repetition. It takes time for new response patterns to form in the brain. You may also wish to set aside *a specific time* each day to focus on your affirmations, such as on awakening or before bedtime.

Turn the final outcome over to a higher power. How many times have you thought you wanted something, only to realize later that having it would have been a major fiasco? For example, a client became forlorn when a home she desired to purchase was sold to another buyer. A year later she discovered the home required $20,000 in hidden repairs. Often we affirm a certain want or desire, when in fact, the universe plans something entirely different—something that is for our higher good. For this reason, I always conclude my affirmations with the following statement: *"This or something better now manifests for me in totally satisfying and harmonious ways for the highest good of all concerned."* This way, I know my will and the will of the universe are aligned.

Techniques for Further Reinforcing Affirmations

Over the years, I have discovered a number of techniques that can reinforce one's affirmations to make them more effective and powerful. The following are some of my favorites:

Use rhyme. Words that rhyme make a more powerful impression on the subconscious mind than blank verse does. The following story illustrates this principle:

> A man suffering from back pain received a healing affirmation from his minister. Soon his condition improved. "I guess that affirmation did the trick," the minister said when he heard the news.
>
> "Well, to tell you the truth," the man replied, "I lost your affirmation the day after you gave it to me."
>
> "How, then, did you heal yourself so quickly?" asked his puzzled minister friend.

The man responded, "Since I couldn't remember your affirmation, I simply told myself, *'Oh hell, I'm well.'*"

Many creative ways to rhyme affirmations exist. Experiment and find your own.

Sing the affirmations to yourself once you create a rhyme. The great Indian poet Tagore said, "God respects me when I pray, but he loves me when I sing."

Make them visible. Place written copies of your affirmations on walls, the car dashboard, the refrigerator, and so on. One woman sticks her affirmations to the bathroom mirror so she sees them each morning and evening.

Make a cassette tape of your affirmation using your own voice. Play the tape as you fall asleep, on awakening, or throughout the day. One of my clients recorded his affirmations for healing and played them on his car stereo during his forty-five-minute commute to work.

Use a mirror. State your affirmation while you look at yourself in the mirror. This is a very powerful way of making contact with yourself.

Incorporate creative visualization with your affirmations. See yourself experiencing the good that you desire in the present moment. Another application of this principle is to make a "treasure map" or "picture of wellness"—a collage of pictures and words that creates a visual presentation of the good you seek (an example appears on page 206).

Human beings have many different ways of perceiving. Thus, when you **say, see,** and **feel** your affirmation, your mental perceptions powerfully combine to produce the optimum result.

Give thanks before or after your affirmation. This is based on the principle that whatever you appreciate grows and expands. The affirmation "I am healthy and well" becomes even more powerful when stated as "I give thanks for my health and wellness." See if you can feel the difference.

Create a notebook or journal. Record your affirmations, noting the date that you write them, so you can keep track of your progress.

Students and clients have tested these techniques over time. I encourage you to incorporate them with your own affirmations.

When Affirmations Don't "Work"

On occasion, the use of affirmations produces mixed results. The following obstacles can block the effectiveness of a good affirmation:

The affirmation is not sufficiently repeated. Remember, repetition is necessary for affirmations to work. You must repeat any new thought pattern many times before it becomes a mental habit.

The affirmation is not specific enough. When a friend at a workshop affirmed "I want more money," the trainer gave him twenty-five cents. Obviously, my friend was asking for a greater amount, but didn't specifically state what that was. It is important to be specific and concrete about what you ask for.

The affirmation lacks a strong feeling element. A nonchalant approach will not work here. Your affirmation must be charged with feeling and intention.

You don't really *believe* the affirmation to be true; in other words, a part of you holds a thought that directly counters the affirmation. Almost everyone who uses affirmations faces this inner resistance. The next section describes dealing with this resistance.

Using Affirmations to Uncover and Transform Negative Beliefs

> One discovers that destiny can be directed, that one does not have to remain in bondage to the first wax imprint made in childhood. One need not be branded by the first pattern.
>
> Once the deforming mirror is smashed, there is a possibility of wholeness; there is a possibility of joy.
>
> —Anaïs Nin

In my work teaching affirmations, I find that affirmations may bring up resistance in the form of negative beliefs from the person's unconscious. For example, suppose you want to work with the affirmation "I am the greatest" (popularized by boxing great Muhammad Ali) to build your self-esteem. But perhaps you have come to believe you are incompetent. Thus, every time you tell yourself how great you are, your subconscious directly contradicts the statement with what it *knows* to be true. A typical dialogue follows.

Conscious Mind	Subconscious Mind
I am the greatest.	I'm afraid you're not.
I am the greatest.	In fact, you're a real loser.
I am the greatest.	You can't do anything right!

The pattern is all too clear. Because your underlying subconscious beliefs portray you as someone who can't get it together, your affirmations fall on deaf ears.

The following is another example, taken from a client suffering from depression:

Conscious Mind	Subconscious Mind
I deserve to be well	Nothing has worked so far.
I deserve to be well.	Depression runs in my family, so I can't avoid it.
I deserve to be well.	I can't afford to seek treatment.

What makes this process so insidious is that you may not even be aware that your subconscious mind sabotages your efforts. Ignoring these subconscious beliefs is like painting over rust or hacking away at weeds without pulling them out by the roots. The basic problem remains unchecked. Despite your best efforts, you remain stuck in the old self-defeating patterns without knowing why.

Fortunately, there is a way out—*bring your subconscious beliefs into conscious awareness;* in other words, expose your most deeply held assumptions about life to the light of day, where you can work with them.

The Affirmation-Dialogue Process

Years ago I learned a simple process that uses affirmations to help one become aware of unconscious limiting beliefs. Here is how it works: Divide a sheet of paper into two columns. Label the left-hand column **"Affirmation"** and the right-hand column **"What Comes Up."**

Affirmation	What Comes Up

Then, after putting yourself in a relaxed and receptive state of mind, write your affirmation in the left-hand column. Afterward be still and notice what bubbles up from the sub-conscious mind. This process is similar to free association. In the right-hand column, write down whatever pops up, no matter how irrelevant it may seem.

After repeating this process six or seven times, the right-hand column should contain a list of the major negative beliefs and assumptions you hold regarding your affirmation. Here is how it worked for Mary, whose goal was to open a fashion boutique specializing in used clothes:

Affirmation	What Comes Up
I am successfully running my own business.	I can't do it.
I am successfully running my own business.	It's too much work.
I am successfully running my own business.	I need to work at a regular nine-to-five job.

I am successfully running my own business.	There's not enough money in it.
I am successfully running my own business.	I need something that provides more security.
I am successfully running my own business.	No one in my family is an entrepreneur.

As you can see, Mary is engaged in a conversation—perhaps "argument" is the more accurate term—with herself. The dispute pits *the desired state*, symbolized by the affirmation, against the *limiting beliefs* of her negative programming and conditioning. The affirmation says *yes* to the desired healing; the negative beliefs respond *no!*

You can represent the essence of the dialogue as follows:

Affirmation	**What Comes Up**
Yes	No
Yes	No
Yes	No

Now that the affirmation-dialogue process has made Mary conscious of her negative beliefs, the next step is to change those no's into yes's so *what she wants* (the conscious mind) can agree with *what she believes she deserves* (the subconscious mind).

Affirmation	**What Comes Up**
Yes	Yes
Yes	Yes
Yes	Yes

You can accomplish this in two ways. In many instances, if a person continues to write down his or her affirmation and record what comes up, the negatives eventually exhaust themselves and positive thoughts and feelings replace them. This is what occurred with Mary as she proceeded:

Affirmation	What Comes Up
I am successfully running my own business.	Maybe it is possible.
I am successfully running my own business.	I have excellent taste in clothing.
I am successfully running my own business.	I know other people who own their own businesses.
I am successfully running my own business.	If they can do it, so can I.
I am successfully running my own business.	With Spirit behind me, all things are possible.

You can see that after Mary became aware of her concerns about starting her own business, they transformed into more hopeful attitudes.

Adding a Third Column

After the publication of my book of affirmations *Words That Heal*, I taught this dialogue process for a number of years. One day, at the conclusion of a seminar, a group of people approached me and complained that they felt overwhelmed by the negative beliefs that came up. Unlike Mary's example, these negative beliefs did not go away with the continued repetition of the affirmation. To remedy this problem, I added another column called the "Second Response," as depicted below:

Affirmation	First Response	Second Response

The function of the Second Response column is to allow the person to *immediately respond* to the limiting belief and set the record straight. Two advantages to this approach exist: Because a lie left unchallenged eventually assumes the aura of truth, quickly responding to the "no" diminishes its power and validity. In addition, replacing the "no" voice with a positive statement makes it less likely that the former will return. If you are a visual person, you can erase the negative picture or scene in your mind's eye and replace it with a positive one.

To illustrate how the process works, let us return to a sample affirmation we used earlier. The affirmation was written by a client named Gary who suffers from depression.

Affirmation	First Response	Second Response
I deserve to be well.	Nothing has worked so far.	
I deserve to be well.	Depression runs in my family, so I can't avoid it.	
I deserve to be well.	I can't afford to seek treatment.	

Having uncovered the negative beliefs in the middle column, Gary can now go back and review them one at a time. In each case, he can ask himself the following:

- Is this statement true?
- How did I obtain this self-defeating belief? Who communicated it to me?
- Do I have anything to say in response to this statement? What can I say to eliminate any falsehoods and set the record straight?

As Gary answers each misperception with the truth about himself, he writes his reply in the "Second Response" column, directly opposite the statement it is meant to replace. The following dialogue shows how he responded to each of his limiting beliefs:

Affirmation	First Response	Second Response
I deserve to be well.	Nothing has worked so far.	Many tools and treatments I have not tried still exist.
I deserve to be well.	Depression runs in my family, so I can't avoid it.	Biology is not destiny. Predispositions can be altered by medications and lifestyle changes.
I deserve to be well.	I can't afford to seek treatment.	Financial assistance is available, including low-cost counseling and free medications from drug companies.

Gary was clearly empowered by confronting his negative beliefs and replacing them with the truth about his situation. As a final step in this process, he took a number of statements from the "Second Response" column and brought them together to create a cohesive declaration of the good he seeks. This is similar to the vision statement described in Appendix C. His example reads as follows:

> I am truly committed to healing from depression. Even though my mother suffered from depression, many new treatments now exist that were not available earlier. I seek these treatments and attract the financial assistance I need to pay for them. Through patience and perseverance, I will reduce my symptoms and restore my brain and nervous system to balance.

On reading these words to himself each day, Gary further reinforces and supports his desire to become well.

Applying the Affirmation-Dialogue Process to Your Own Issues

Take a moment and reflect on a specific goal you have for recovering from depression or a mood disorder. One simple way to create a goal is to take a current symptom (for example, poor sleep) and turn it into its opposite (sound, restful sleep). Thus the problem of low self-esteem becomes the goal of "healthy self-esteem," the problem of difficulty making decisions becomes the goal of "improvement in decision making," and so on. Your goal will probably focus on a change in your thinking, your feelings, your physical well-being, or your behaviors. (If you worked with my book *Healing from Depression*, you can choose a goal from the goal sheet you filled out on page 151.)

Once you identify your goal, create an affirmation with a message that contains a *resolution* of that challenge (for example, if your goal is increased exercise, you might use the affirmation "I now work out at the gym three times a week"). Use the guidelines stated at the beginning of this chapter to formulate your affirmation. Write your recovery goal and its healing affirmation below or on a separate piece of paper:

My healing goal (a change in a thought, feeling, behavior, or aspect of your physiology):

_____

_____

The affirmation for bringing this goal to fruition:

_____

_____

Now it is time to work with the affirmation in depth. Start by repeating it to yourself throughout the day. Write your affirmation down, and post it in your home where you can see it on a regular basis.

In addition, use the affirmation-dialogue process so your unconscious negative beliefs can surface and be released. If a particular deep-seated belief or complex continues to persist, you may need to seek out a therapist, counselor, priest, minister, rabbi, or so on—someone who can serve as a guide to assist you through the process of growth and change.

When working with the affirmation-dialogue process, let your intuition guide you. You don't have to refute every statement in the middle column. Just respond when it feels appropriate. Experience how empowering it feels to give yourself the support you deserve. No matter how strong your conditioning may be, it is possible to transmute your negative beliefs into positive ones. You'll be amazed at how quickly you can change old beliefs when you end the internal dialogue on an affirmative note.

The Daily Lessons

❧

Look to this day!
For it is life, the very life of life.
In its brief course
Lie all the verities and realities of your existence:
  The bliss of growth;
  The glory of action;
  The splendor of achievement;
For yesterday is but a dream,
And tomorrow but a vision;
But today, well lived, makes every yesterday
  a dream of happiness,
And every tomorrow a vision of hope.
Look well, therefore, to this day!

—"Kalidasa," an ancient Sanskrit poem

Here are thirty-one daily lessons for healing from depression and other mood disorders. Each lesson includes the following:

1. **The daily meditation**—a short passage that focuses on one of the five areas of my "better mood recovery program" as described in my book *Healing from Depression*. These areas are physical self-care, mental/emotional self-care, social support, spiritual connection, and lifestyle habits.

2. **A series of affirmations**—positive thoughts and ideas on which you consciously focus to produce a desired result. When repeated, each day's affirmations will help

you internalize the day's lesson so the greatest amount of healing may take place.

3. A quotation that encapsulates the essence of the day's lesson.

4. A self-care activity that contains a healing idea or behavior that you can apply during the day.

As the poem at the beginning of this chapter describes, the goal of these lessons is to manage your moods, one day at a time. To get the most out of this material, you need the following:

- A comfortable spot in your environment (If you make a habit of meditating, use your normal meditation area. Otherwise, find a space where no one will disturb you for a period of time.)
- A blank notebook or three-ring binder with paper that you can use as a journal

At the beginning of the day: Sit down in your quiet space with your journal, and turn to the lesson for the day. You can choose today's lesson in one of two ways.

One possibility is to begin with the lesson that corresponds to the current day of the month. For example, if it were July 17, you would turn to the lesson for Day 17 and continue reading one lesson per day until the end of the month. Then, on the first day of August, turn to Day 1 and continue to read each subsequent lesson on its corresponding day until you reach August 31. Then begin on Day 1 again, and so on through each month. Using this method, there will be some months (the months with less than thirty-one days) where you will not cover all thirty-one lessons.

The second option is to begin with Day 1 regardless of what day of the month it is. Thus, even if today were May 22, you would still start with Day 1, then continue through, working with one lesson each day. If you miss a day, pick up where you left off. After you reach Day 31, turn back to Day 1 to begin the cycle anew.

Having chosen your daily lesson, read the entire passage—the meditation, the affirmations, the quote or quotes, and the self-care activity. Pay attention to whatever insights or emotional states arise. You may wish to write these down in your journal.

During the day: As the day unfolds, do the self-care activity that follows the affirmations. This activity helps you apply the principle of the daily lesson. If time doesn't permit, that's all right. Continue to read through the lessons each day. You can always come back to the activity in the following month.

At the end of the day: At the end of your day, I invite you to reflect back on the day's events. If the daily lesson, affirmations, quote, or self-care activity had a special impact on you, record your thoughts and impressions in your recovery journal.

In addition, you may wish to record your average mood for the day using the mood scale on page 30.

Use this scale to assign a numerical value to your mood, ranging from –5 to +5. I find that the simple act of observing my moods and giving them a rating allows me to be more objective about them. In addition, tracking my daily mood helps me observe my progress toward recovery and lets me know when I might be slipping.

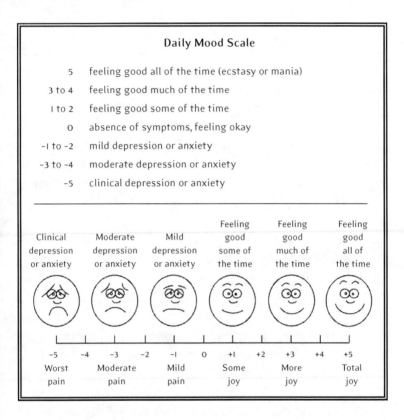

Daily Mood Scale

5	feeling good all of the time (ecstasy or mania)
3 to 4	feeling good much of the time
1 to 2	feeling good some of the time
0	absence of symptoms, feeling okay
-1 to -2	mild depression or anxiety
-3 to -4	moderate depression or anxiety
-5	clinical depression or anxiety

Clinical depression or anxiety	Moderate depression or anxiety	Mild depression or anxiety	Feeling good some of the time	Feeling good much of the time	Feeling good all of the time

-5	-4	-3	-2	-1	0	+1	+2	+3	+4	+5
Worst pain		Moderate pain		Mild pain		Some joy		More joy		Total joy

I encourage you to read a lesson a day for a month and see what happens. If this process makes a difference for you, repeat the lessons for another month, and continue to cycle through the material as long as you want to. My hope is that you will feel better, knowing that you are actively engaged in bringing about your healing.

Now, let's begin.

Setting the Intention to Heal

The Taoist philosopher Lao Tsu once said, "The journey of a thousand miles begins with a single step." Today you set out on a journey of healing from the blues. What is your first step as you begin this quest? It is simply to state your intention to get well.

This may seem like a simple act, but profound ramifications for your future health and well-being exist. By setting the intention to heal, you stimulate and support your body's "healing system"—its innate capacity to restore wellness and bring itself back into balance. It doesn't matter how long you have suffered. You don't have to know *how* your healing will take place; you don't even have to *believe* it is possible. Just ask yourself, "Does a part of me, even if it is 10 percent or 1 percent, want to feel better?" If you can find just a molecule within you that says, "I want to heal," your journey has begun.

Like an arrow flying toward a target, intention is clear, specific, and has the power of commitment behind it. It is this one-pointed commitment that activates a benevolent aspect of the universe that will draw to you the resources, people, and circumstances to bring about your healing. In other words, if you can take the first step toward your goal of healing, the universe takes ten steps back toward you. Help exists from seen and unseen forces. This help will be made available once you set the intention to heal.

Healing Affirmations

1. Today I set the intention to heal.
2. I release the past and eagerly look toward the good that awaits me.
3. I am the person responsible for my health and well-being.
4. As I take steps to help myself, I activate the benevolent forces that help bring about my healing.
5. I envision myself in a better mood.
6. Write your own affirmation.

Words to Consider

Whatever you can do, or dream you can, begin it.
Boldness has genius, power and magic in it.

—Goethe

Self-Care Activity for Day 1

An important part of setting the intention to heal is writing down your vision of wellness—a specific mental blueprint or picture of the state of health that you seek to bring into your life. To formulate your vision of wellness, ask yourself the following questions:

- What would my life look and feel like if I were free from my symptoms?
- How would my body look and feel? How much physical energy would I have?
- How would I feel most of the time? What types of thoughts would I think?
- What types of relationships would I have? What kind of work would I be involved in? What would my spiritual life be like?

Drawing on the answers to the above questions, on a separate page, write a paragraph (or more) describing your vision of mental and emotional health. See if you can use all five senses—sight, hearing, touch, smell, and taste—to depict your experience. Write it in the present tense, as if the experience were happening now.

Once you write your vision of wellness, read it every day as a part of your healing process. Repeating your vision statement on a regular basis makes it a part of your consciousness and your life. If you would like to read over some sample vision statements, please turn to Appendix C.

Day 2

Reaching Out for Support

The journey of healing from the blues is not a solo flight. To fully manifest your intention to heal, you need the help and support of other people. The success of Alcoholics Anonymous demonstrates this principle of mutual support. No cure existed for alcoholism until two drunks came together and said, "Let's do together what neither of us can do alone." In a similar fashion, support is an essential ingredient in healing from depression and other mood disorders. It takes a whole village to shepherd someone through a dark night of the soul.

Human beings are wired for connection. Social scientists have documented that love and intimacy provide a major buffer against stress, reduce mental decline, bolster the immune system, and contribute to longevity. In addition, when you state your intention to heal in the presence of others so other people's attention focuses on your goal, that intention becomes strengthened and exponentially magnified. Moreover, times arise when you may feel too discouraged to believe that recovery is possible. During these periods, other members of a support team can hold a vision of your healing when you cannot do so yourself. (This is also called "keeping the high watch.")

You can draw on many sources of support, such as family and friends, mental health professionals, mentors and allies, support groups, and pets and animal friends. Unfortunately, many who suffer from depression and other mood disorders feel ashamed, shy, or undeserving of help or don't want to feel like a burden to others. If asking for assistance seems hard, please consider that most people *enjoy* being of support. By giving to you, they also give to themselves.

If asking for help still seems difficult, please reconsider calling *someone*, even if it is a crisis line. Reaching out *will* make a real difference in your recovery. I promise.

Healing Affirmations

1. I let go of my resistance to asking for help. I realize that I do not have to carry my burden alone.
2. I am worthy of accepting other people's assistance.
3. I take steps to ask others for help.
4. I allow myself to receive other people's support.
5. My burden lightens when it is borne with a friend.
6. Write your own affirmation.

Words to Consider

Anything that promotes a sense of isolation
often leads to illness and suffering.

Anything that promotes a sense of love and intimacy,
connection and community, is healing.

—*Dean Ornish,* Love and Survival

Self-Care Activity for Day 2

Today ask yourself, "How well do I connect with social support in my life?" In your recovery journal, list any family members, friends, mentors, health professionals, and support group members (or pets) to whom you can turn for companionship and support.

Pick one of these people, and share with him or her that you are reading this book. Ask if he or she would be willing to hold the image of your vision statement with you or if he or she has anything to add to it.

One Day at a Time

❧

One of the most important ways to heal from the blues is to live one day at a time. Life feels much less overwhelming when you approach it in manageable twenty-four-hour chunks. Moreover, because emotional states are transitory, each day that you cope brings you one step closer to healing.

Living one day at a time becomes possible when you structure your day so it is filled with a series of simple, doable events. Feelings of anxiety decrease when you know what is immediately in front of you. For example, you might begin your day by writing in your journal, followed by eating breakfast, taking a thirty-minute walk, and going to the community center to socialize. By stringing together a series of short-term activities, you fill the day. Or perhaps a job provides the structure you need. And when evening comes, take heart in knowing that you made it through another twenty-four-hour period.

Even during a well-planned day, you may feel fearful at times about the future or ruminate about the past. If this occurs, notice that you have wandered from the present, and then refocus your attention on the here and now. Do this by calling a friend or counselor, going on a walk, taking a deep breath, saying "This, too, shall pass," and so on. Notice how your distress subsides when you shift your attention away from the future to the here and now.

Right now your job—your focus—is to develop a series of coping strategies to get you through the day, hour by hour, minute by minute, until the pattern of your condition shifts. Because the only constant in the physical universe is change, such a shift will likely occur. Practice living one day at a time, and change will happen when you least expect it.

Healing Affirmations

1. My job today is to focus on the present.
2. I am making it through this difficult period.
3. I can handle focusing on today.
4. Each new day brings me closer to recovery.
5. I am creating the support I need to get through this situation, one day at a time.
6. Write your own affirmation.

Words to Consider

Yard by yard, life is hard;
Inch by inch, it's a cinch.

—Proverb

Self-Care Activity for Day 3

Today pay attention to your thoughts, and notice how much you live in the present. If you observe your mind worrying about the future or obsessing about the past, gently return your focus to the here and now.

Living one day at a time becomes easier when your day has structure. Make a list of simple, doable, low-cost activities that work for you. Examples include working on a jigsaw puzzle, performing a prayer ritual, listening to music, going to the community center, hiking in nature, writing in a journal, calling or spending time with a friend, and so on. It is important to pay particular attention to planning weekends, because they are more likely to contain a lack of structured time.

Physical Self-Care: The Starting Point of Recovery

Today, we will focus on the starting point of healing from the blues—taking care of the physical body. When you feel great physically—full of vitality, energetic, awake, alert, and so on—it is almost impossible to be in a bad mood. As my friend who suffers from anxiety is fond of saying, "It is so much easier to be positive and calm after a good night's sleep!"

Another reason to focus on physical health is that it deals with the most basic human needs—food, water, air, sleep, touch, and movement. Because these needs are so elemental, many people take them for granted. But when you ignore your basic needs, the entire body—as well as your mood—gets thrown out of balance.

Unfortunately, many of us grew up with negative body images. We did not like how we looked or how our bodies performed. We became ashamed of our bodies. This self-loathing can lead you to engage in unhealthy health habits (such as eating unhealthy foods, not getting adequate sleep, and so on) that contribute to the syndrome of depression and other mood disorders.

Take a moment and ask yourself, "How do I treat my body? Do I provide it with adequate amounts of food, water, exercise, fresh air, and rest? When my body is sick, do I slow down or do I become angry with it for interfering with my plans? When did I last give myself a massage or some other sensual pleasure?"

Now express appreciation to your body for all that it gives you. Ask your body what it needs right now, and then fulfill its request. Your body is your ally in mental health recovery. When you love and respect your body, you love and respect yourself.

Healing Affirmations

1. I am thankful for being here in this body.
2. I take good care of my body to help myself.
3. My body is a source of pleasure and strength.
4. My body is healthy, strong, and radiant.
5. I give my body love for all that it does for me.
6. Write your own affirmation.

Words to Consider

If anything is sacred, the human body is sacred.

—Walt Whitman

Self-Care Activity for Day 4

Turn to the diagram on page 7, called Healing from Depression and Anxiety: Five Areas of Therapeutic Self-Care. Read through the activities listed under the heading "Physical Self-Care" and note which ones appeal to you. Then commit to doing one or more activities today. If you enjoy it, you might want to make it a part of your daily routine, if you do not already do so.

In addition, write down the physical self-care strategies you currently practice in your life. Give yourself credit for the ways you take care of yourself.

Your Body Was Made to Move

Exercise—any physical activity that promotes endurance, flexibility, or strengthening—is a natural mood elevator. The latest scientific research demonstrates that as little as three hours a week of regular exercise reduces the symptoms of mild to moderate depression as effectively as Prozac and other medications. Aerobic exercise in particular improves circulation, brings increased blood flow and oxygen to the brain, and releases endorphins, the body's natural painkilling chemicals. The only "side effects" of aerobic exercise are a stronger cardiovascular system and better overall health.

Regular exercise has become the central pillar of my recovery program. On weekdays I ride my stationary bike and swim in the evening. On weekends I take long walks in the forest. When I miss my routines for even one or two days, I am more likely to become depressed or anxious. When I return to my schedule, the self-doubts, fears, and anxieties melt away.

One reason many people resist exercise is that they see it as something arduous and unpleasant. To heal this resistance, see if you can turn the *e* in exercise to the *e* in enjoy. In other words, strive to make exercise fun by connecting it to activities that give you pleasure. Such activities might include the following:

- gardening
- hiking in nature
- dancing—that is, jazzercise, folk dancing, and so on
- planned activities with friends, such as shooting basketball, playing tennis, or throwing a Frisbee with the dog
- an exercise videotape at home

Your body was made to move. Whether it is a daily walk in the park, a water aerobics or yoga class, or dancing to your favorite music, get into motion. Start with small steps, and remind yourself that you don't have to be perfect. At the pool where I swim, I see many disabled, elderly, and overweight people taking part in water exercise classes. Even if you have a physical disability or carry extra pounds, it is usually possible to engage in some form of movement.

Healing Affirmations

1. Today I celebrate the joy of movement.
2. I find the time to exercise on a regular basis, even if I have a busy schedule.
3. I find activities that are fun and enjoyable to do.
4. I attract the people I need to help make my exercise regimen a success.
5. The more I move my body, the better I feel.
6. Write your own affirmation.

Words to Consider

A certain portion of every day should be set aside for exercise. If the body is weak, the mind will not be strong.

–Thomas Jefferson

Self-Care Activity for Day 5

Today take inventory of your relationship with exercise. Think about what types of physical activities make your body feel good. Take one of these exercise activities, and commit to doing it today. You can also choose mundane activities that give you a natural workout. These include the following:

- doing the laundry
- walking up the stairs in your office building
- walking to the grocery store
- yard work, such as pruning roses, edging the lawn, and pulling weeds
- parking a few blocks from your destination and walking the remaining distance
- planting and harvesting vegetables
- having physical activity incorporated into your job (See if there is a place at work where you could do some stretches and exercises on your break.)

If you enjoy your exercise activity, you may want to make it a part of your daily routine, if you do not already do so. Remember, any exercise that you bring into your daily life is a support on the path to recovery.

Taking the Time to Breathe

One of the most powerful ways to impact the emotions and mood is through the breath. In Sanskrit, the word for breath is *prana*, which also means "life" or "spirit." How you breathe both reflects and influences the state of the nervous system, directly impacting your mood and sense of well-being. For example, when you become anxious or fearful, you tend to breathe shallowly and rapidly. Racing thoughts and out-of-control worries usually accompany this rapid breathing. An effective way to lessen these thoughts is to decrease your rate of breathing. As you inhale slowly and deeply, notice how your thoughts slow down. It may also help to hold yourself—place one hand on your belly and another on your heart as you breathe. Experiment with finding a physical posture that feels soothing and nurturing.

Abdominal breathing (also called *diaphragmatic breathing*) involves using your entire chest and abdominal cavity to breathe. Here is a brief description of the process, which you can try *right now*.

Sit in a comfortable position with your spine straight (you can also lie on your back). Place both hands on your abdomen, right beneath your rib cage, with the fingers of the hands spread out and just touching each other. Now inhale slowly and deeply, sending the air as low down in your chest as you can. Feel as if you are pushing the air downward toward your tummy. As your belly fills up with air, you should notice that the fingers of your two hands slowly *move apart*.

After you take a full breath, pause momentarily and exhale slowly through your nose or mouth. As you do so, you will see your abdomen deflating, much like a balloon that is losing its air. Let your body go limp as you watch your hands on your abdomen slowly return to their original position. Your fingers should touch again.

Try repeating this eight to ten times, breathing deeply and slowly without gulping in air or letting it all out at once. You may wish to count to four on the inhale and to eight on the exhale (or whatever rhythm works best for you).

Healing Affirmations

1. Today I will take the time to breathe. Breathing deeply from my diaphragm brings oxygen to my brain and body, giving me energy and mental focus.
2. I slow down my breathing to slow down my thoughts.
3. As I breathe deeply, I feel more relaxed.
4. Taking deep breaths helps me feel more vital and alive.
5. My breathing connects me to Spirit.
6. Write your own affirmation.

Words to Consider

Things to Do Today:

1. Inhale . . . exhale.
2. Inhale . . . exhale.
3. Inhale . . . exhale.

Self-Care Activity for Day 6

Today take one or two periods to practice abdominal breathing. This is especially useful if you feel anxious or seek a way to disengage from racing or obsessive thoughts. Also observe your breath as a way of taking a time out in the midst of a busy day or stopping to refresh yourself when you feel overly tired.

Day 7

Making Your Mind Your Friend

In the past few days, you learned how changing your physiology through physical self-care can lead to a better mood. A second way to change the way you feel is to change your thoughts. Every thought that you and I think produces a chemical reaction in the brain, which in turn gives rise to a feeling. As one brain scientist explained it, every thought has a neurochemical equivalent!

Imagine that two people at work on Friday look out the window and observe that it is raining. The first, who hoped to play golf over the weekend, feels disappointed and moans, "This rain is depressing." The second remarks, "I'm so pleased. This means snow will exist in the mountains, and I can take my family skiing." Is the rain a good thing or a bad thing? It all depends on how you think about it.

Unfortunately, many people tend to interpret the world in pessimistic ways, with a negative view of themselves, the world, and their future. This tendency to "see through a glass darkly" is caused by "cognitive distortions," which are automatic negative thought patterns that distort the truth of who you are. Examples of these thinking errors are statements such as "I'm worthless," "I'll probably blow it," and "If I don't do it perfectly, I'm a failure." When thoughts like these repeat over a period of time, they produce feelings of loneliness, alienation, stress, anger, helplessness, distrust, and fear.

The process of "cognitive restructuring" involves challenging these beliefs and replacing them with more rational and realistic beliefs. This process takes commitment and hard work and time. But the rewards are clear. When you change the nature of your thinking, you change your brain's biochemistry and ultimately your mood.

Healing Affirmations

1. My mind is a powerful tool.
2. I can use my mind to heal myself.
3. As the writer and director of my own movie, I can change the script.
4. I fill my mind with positive and uplifting thoughts.
5. I deserve to be happy.
6. Write your own affirmation.

Words to Consider

The mind is its own place, and in itself can
make a Heav'n of Hell or a Hell of Heav'n.

—*John Milton*, Paradise Lost

Self-Care Activity for Day 7

The following table contains a list of thinking errors and negative core beliefs that are linked to depression and low self-esteem. Many of these negative thoughts and beliefs formed in early childhood when parents, teachers, relatives, religious upbringing, and television all gave you a model of *who you were* and *how the world worked.*

Take a moment and ask yourself, "What kind of negative thoughts and beliefs do I hold?" and write the answers in your journal. Opposite each negative core belief, write a more empowering thought or belief about yourself or the world. For example, you can replace the belief "Life is only about suffering" with "Life contains times of joy."

Negative Core Beliefs

About Myself:

- I must earn love.
- I'm not lovable.
- I'm incompetent.
- I'm not important.
- I'm not creative.
- I must please others.
- I don't fit in.
- My opinions don't count.
- I'm a bad person.
- I can't do it.
- I'm not as smart as others.
- I'm clumsy.
- I'm ugly.
- I am a failure.
- I don't deserve to succeed.
- I can't have what I want.
- I don't deserve happiness.
- I can't be myself.
- It's not okay to show my feelings.

About the World:

- The world is unhappy.
- Nice guys finish last.
- Life's a bitch and then you die.
- The world is against me.

About Relationships:

- I'll never find the right person.
- I can't trust men/women.
- If I love, I'll be hurt.
- I can't make it without my partner.
- My partner can't make it without me.
- I must control my partner.
- Relationships can't last.
- The one I love will abandon me.

Day 8

Accentuate the Positive

O ne of your most powerful allies in improving your mood is in the ability to choose your attitude. The reason your attitude is so important is that how you perceive the world directly affects how you feel. We are taught to believe that events cause us to have certain feelings. But evidence shows that our interpretation of an event, or how we think about it, elicits our feelings. When we accentuate the positive, a corresponding chemical change occurs in the brain that leads to a better mood.

My favorite story about the power of attitude concerns two brothers—Davey the optimist and Joey the pessimist. The parents were tired of always seeing Davey cheerful and Joey gloomy, so they arranged a unique experiment. For Joey, they purchased a Shetland pony, and for Davey, a room full of horse manure. They left the boys alone with their new presents and checked back with them an hour later. True to form, Joey was whining away. "The horse isn't the right color; the saddle is too big," he moaned. It seemed that nothing could satisfy him.

The parents then turned their attention to Davey, expecting him to be in the same melancholic state. Instead, they found him enthusiastically diving into and playing with the manure.

"What's going on?" they inquired. "How can you feel happy with such a yucky birthday present?"

"Don't you see?" Davey replied. "With all of this horse poop around, there must be a pony hiding somewhere."

Choosing to accentuate the positive, while simple in theory, is not always easy to practice. When a person becomes severely depressed, the disruption in the brain's biochemistry makes it impossible to hold a positive thought for any length of time. In such cases, direct physical interventions such as antidepressants or spiritual interventions such as prayer may be required. If your condition makes it hard for you to stay positive, try to be patient and gentle with yourself. You are doing the best you can.

Once you feel better, consciously practice optimistic ways of thinking until they become a mental habit. Remember, every thought leads to a neurochemical change in the brain. Cultivating an optimistic attitude reaps benefits both in your current mood and in helping to prevent a future downturn in your mood.

Healing Affirmations

1. I have the capacity to feel better.
2. I am taking steps to help myself feel better.
3. While I cannot always control my circumstances, I can choose how I respond to them.
4. I can reframe a situation to focus on the positive.
5. I am cultivating an optimistic way of thinking.
6. Write your own affirmation.

Words to Consider

Everything can be taken away from a man but one thing: the last of the human freedoms—to choose one's attitude in any given set of circumstances, to choose one's own way.

—*Victor Frankl,* Man's Search for Meaning

Self-Care Activity for Day 8

Today observe how you perceive your world. Do you tend to see the glass as half empty or half full? Do you seek to emphasize what is positive in your life or focus on the pain? During the day, practice the following:

1. **Become aware when your mind engages in negative thinking.** Identify the self-defeating negative thought or self-statement. Then say the words "Cancel! Cancel!" aloud.
2. **Replace the negative thought with a more realistic and supportive thought or belief.** Then note how you feel. (Find more information on how to do this in my book *Healing from Depression: 12 Weeks to a Better Mood* or David Burns's *Feeling Good.*)

Blessings in Disguise

Yesterday you learned about your ability to choose your attitude in any given situation. Practicing this skill is especially important during times of adversity. Fortunately, a spiritual law exists that states *"every challenge, difficulty, or defeat contains within it the seed of an equivalent or greater good."* How can you find this hidden blessing?

The first step is to dive into the experience and fully feel the painful feelings. Trying to "get over it" and get on with your life by staying upbeat is the equivalent of denial. Moreover, a universal principle states that "whatever you resist persists." Repressing or avoiding painful feelings only intensifies them. Instead, you must allow yourself to experience the pain, grief, anger, and so on that are natural responses to a loss or setback.

Once you fully *embrace* your feelings, you are ready for the next step, which is to look for some unexpected benefit or blessing. This blessing may not be apparent in the midst of the challenge; often it is revealed after you emerge from your ordeal.

Lance Armstrong was a well-known American cyclist when he developed testicular cancer at the age of twenty-seven. The cancer was a horrendous experience that almost killed him. Yet, in retrospect, Armstrong says that getting cancer helped him win five consecutive Tour de France bicycle races. "Before I faced cancer, I was on cruise control," Armstrong recalls. "Cancer taught me to fight and to persevere. Without those lessons, I would not have become a champion." Ironically, the cancer gave Armstrong a second gift by taking pounds off his upper body. His lighter weight and the reduction in his wind resistance made him a faster rider.

Armstrong's story illustrates the paradox that the worst thing that ever happens to you can also be the best thing that ever happened. Unwanted, difficult circumstances can lead to unexpected good.

Healing Affirmations

1. Life is a school with many valuable teachings.
2. Behind every dark cloud lies a rainbow.
3. All things are working for good in my life.
4. I have the patience and the strength to bear this pain; I trust that some good will come of it.
5. I can learn from every situation I encounter.
6. Write your own affirmation.

Words to Consider

When written in Chinese, the word "crisis"
is composed of two characters.

One represents danger, and the other represents opportunity.

—John F. Kennedy

Self-Care Activity for Day 9

Today see if you can practice the art of "reframing" by looking for the inherent advantage in any situation. Below, find two exercises to get you started.

To begin, look back at your life, and find an event or circumstance in the past in which something painful occurred that afterward led to an unexpected good. First write about the event and then the positive outcome that occurred afterward (for example, you lost one job only to find a better one).

Next, pick a current situation or circumstance that you find challenging. See if you can step back and put a new "frame" around it so you can look at it from a new perspective.

If the challenge you picked is your current mood disorder, ask yourself if any lessons, teachings, or gains have emerged from your experience. (For example, my depression has made me more compassionate to others in pain.) Has any personal or spiritual growth occurred? If all you can see is the horse poop and not the pony (see Davey's story on Day 8), ask that a blessing be revealed. If you are open to receiving such a blessing, you will be more likely to find it.

Day 10

An Attitude of Gratitude

In the past two lessons, you learned the value of accentuating the positive and looking for hidden blessings in your life. A powerful way to do this is to practice gratitude. When you give thanks, you automatically focus your attention on what works in your life instead of what does not work. This shift in perspective actually changes brain chemistry and counteracts negative thinking.

What would it be like if you began each day by asking, *"What is beneficial in my life right now? What can I be grateful for? What or who works to support me in my health and healing?"* If you think long enough, you might identify a few simple blessings, such as "The sun is shining," "I have a roof over my head," "I have enough to eat," "My body is in reasonable health," "I have a good friend," "I feel love for my child," and so on.

Expressing gratitude does not mean denying pain or uncomfortable feelings. It doesn't mean pretending something is wonderful that clearly isn't. But when you focus exclusively on those dark and painful places, you close yourself to the good that is present.

As you spend time each day giving thanks and feeling grateful, you begin to uncover life's blessings, even during difficult times. The following story illustrates how this insight led the great Zen master Banzan to enlightenment.

One day while walking in the marketplace, Banzan overheard a conversation between a butcher and his customer:

"Give me the best piece of meat you have," said the customer.

"Every piece of meat I have is the best," the butcher replied. "There is no piece of meat here that is not the best."

On hearing this, Banzan became enlightened; that is, he realized that every moment in life, despite its imperfections, contains something for which to be grateful.

Healing Affirmations

1. I am grateful for the blessings I experience in my life.

2. I am blessed in many ways.

3. I improve how I feel by focusing on what works well in my life.

4. Giving thanks in the midst of a painful situation helps alleviate the pain.

5. Every experience provides an opportunity to grow in love and wisdom.

6. Write your own affirmation.

Words to Consider

Count your blessings, not your crosses,
Count your gains, not your losses.
Count your joys instead of your woes,
Count your friends instead of your foes.
Covet your health, not your wealth.

—Proverb

Self-Care Activity for Day 10

Today take inventory of all for which you have to be thankful. With a timer set on five minutes, speed write a list of everything in your life that you appreciate. Write down whatever comes to mind, no matter how silly or irrelevant it seems. When you finish, your list will no doubt include simple items as well as bigger ones.

When you complete the list, transfer it to your recovery journal. Before you go to sleep, fill yourself with a feeling of thankfulness. You may want to place something by your bed (an object, a photograph, an affirmation, and so on) that helps instill a feeling of gratitude.

The Self-Talk Solution

As Jodi Foster accepted her first Oscar for her performance as an actress in a motion picture, she thanked her mother for telling her "that all of my finger paintings were Picassos and that there was nothing to be afraid of." Those words, spoken to Jodi at an early age, gave her the confidence and belief in herself that translated into two Academy Awards.

As Jodi's story demonstrates, each word or phrase you say to yourself carries with it an *underlying message* about who you are and your relationship with the world. Once you internalize this message, it becomes a belief that governs your future experience. Even if you are not conscious of the belief, it nevertheless affects all aspects of your life.

A successful entrepreneur reported that when he was four years old, his mother sat beside him at bedtime and whispered into his ear, "You can do anything you want. There are no limits to what you can achieve." Having heard this affirmation thousands of times, Nathan was a confident child who believed in pursuing his dreams. In his midtwenties, he started his own boat-building business, which developed into a highly successful enterprise. Now he uses the same affirmative phrases with his children.

Whether you heard words of praise or words of criticism when you were a child, it is your responsibility as an adult to speak to yourself in a loving and compassionate manner. Take a look at your own self-talk. Do you speak to yourself with a "yes voice" (the voice that affirms and encourages) or a "no voice" (the voice of doubt, worry, anxiety, limitation, shame, and self-contempt)? Clearly, the more your self-talk arises out of the "yes voice," the healthier your mood will be.

Through the power of your thoughts and words, you have the ability to shape your inner and outer reality. When you learn to speak to yourself in loving and kind ways, you change your thinking, thereby changing your mood.

Healing Affirmations

1. I monitor my self-talk on a daily basis.
2. I am careful about what I put into my mental computer.
3. I fill my mind with positive, nurturing, and healing thoughts.
4. I surround myself with positive ideas, people, and environments.
5. I speak words that uplift, bless, and heal.
6. Write your own affirmation.

Words to Consider

If you think you can, you can.
If you think you can't, you can't.
Either way you are right.

—Henry Ford

Self-Care Activity for Day 11

Close your eyes. Go back in time, and picture a moment in your life in which you felt proud or good about yourself. Perhaps you were engaged in a positive action, someone gave you a compliment, or you reflected on one of your strengths. Choose an adjective (such as kind, creative, courageous, and so on) that describes yourself in that moment.

Next, use this adjective to complete the following sentences:

1. I am _____.
2. *(State your name)*, you are _____.*

For example, if I saw myself as courageous, my affirmations would be as follows: (1) *I am courageous;* and (2) *Douglas, you are courageous.*

As you read your affirmation aloud, note how it feels to say something positive *about* yourself and *to* yourself. Does it bring up any feelings of resistance or unworthiness?

I also recommend that you give your affirmation to a friend and ask him or her to repeat it back to you in the second person—for example, my partner would say to me, *"Douglas, you are courageous."* Ask yourself again, "What feelings come up when I hear this positive self-statement from another person?"

Finally, if you want to increase the effectiveness of your affirmation, repeat it while *looking in the mirror.* Although this may feel uncomfortable, combining the visual and auditory senses will boost this affirmation's potency.

* Repeat this exercise as many times as you wish to create a series of positive affirmations for yourself.

Taming the Inner Critic

It is a common observation that people who suffer from depression and other mood disorders also suffer from low self-esteem. A huge contributor to low self-worth is the negative inner voice that constantly judges, criticizes, negates, and attacks you. This voice is often called the "inner critic." Some of the inner critic's favorite tactics are as follows:

- blaming you for things that go wrong
- comparing you to others' achievements and abilities and finding you wanting
- keeping track of your failures, but never once reminding you of your strengths and abilities
- calling you names—stupid, incompetent, weak, selfish, defective, ugly—and making you believe they are all true
- setting impossible standards of perfection and hounding you for the smallest mistake

The inner critic is usually some internalized critical parent or other authority who judged, criticized, or put you down when you were a child. Now is the time to take back your power.

Ultimately, the best way to inoculate yourself against the inner critic is to practice self-acceptance. The inner critic's power comes from the belief that you are not okay the way you are. Once you start to feel compassion for yourself and practice self-forgiveness, the inner critic's influence over you will diminish. Because the inner critic's patterns are often deep-seated, changing the patterns may require outside help such as counseling or medication.

Healing Affirmations

1. I am a person with talents and gifts.
2. The voice of the inner critic falls on deaf ears.
3. When I feel down, it is important for me to be gentle with myself.
4. Each day I notice, accept, and appreciate myself for who I am and what I do.
5. I am a good person who deserves love and happiness.
6. Write your own affirmation.

Words to Consider

Nobody can make you feel inferior without your permission.

—*Eleanor Roosevelt*

Self-Care Activity for Day 12

Today pay attention to your self-talk, and notice if you hear any stirrings of the inner critic. If you notice that you put yourself down, compare yourself to others, use the word "should," or set impossible standards of perfection, you can be sure the inner critic is at work. The following is a simple, three-step process to help you get started in taming the inner critic:

First, become aware of the existence of the inner critic. It helps to give the inner critic a name—such as the bully, the critic, the judge, Mr./Ms. Perfect, a parent's name, Mr./Ms. Kick-Ass, Hard-Ass and so on. This helps give you some distance from this critic.

Next, halt what the critic says. After becoming aware of the critic's voice, you can short-circuit the negative self-talk and stop it in its tracks. Words and phrases designed to do that include the following: "Stop that!" "Shut up!" "Cancel, cancel!" "Lies, lies, and more lies," "I beg to disagree, Mother," "I beg to disagree, Father," "I beg to disagree, *(fill in a name)*."

Finally, replace the critic's negative self-talk with a more realistic and compassionate view of yourself. If the inner critic engages in outright put-downs, take the negative statement and turn it into its opposite. For example, you can change the phrase "What a jerk!" to "I'm okay," or you can change "You're stupid" to "I'm intelligent."

If you practice this technique on a regular basis, your nurturing adult gradually will replace the inner critic.

Self-Forgiveness

Yesterday we spoke of the inner critic and how he/she loves to put us down. One of the inner critic's favorite tactics is to blame us for our past mistakes. Examples of such mishaps include dropping out of school, going off medication and having a relapse, getting into drugs and alcohol, becoming involved in an unhealthy relationship, or passing up a golden business opportunity. Although part of life involves making and learning from mistakes, you may have the tendency to "beat yourself up" and hold yourself in contempt, even if the incident occurred thirty to forty years ago. Such self-blame and guilt further debilitate a person's damaged self-esteem.

Healing from depression and other mental disorders means releasing this self-blame and learning to forgive yourself. You can have compassion for yourself by seeing that you do the best you can with the awareness you have at the time. Accepting that you truly are doing your best lifts a huge burden from your shoulders and psyche. You literally feel lighter as feelings of guilt and heaviness release.

Ask yourself today, "Are there any areas in my life in which I have not forgiven myself for mistakes I made in the past? Am I open to seeing that perhaps I did the best I could at the time with the awareness I had?" Have compassion for yourself for whatever pain you caused yourself or others. Have mercy on yourself. Allow yourself to be forgiven. Allow yourself to heal.

The process of self-forgiveness is not an easy one, nor does it occur overnight. If you wish to pursue self-forgiveness in greater depth, I suggest that you work with a trained counselor or spiritual advisor. Excellent books and resources on forgiveness also exist that will help you in your process.

Healing Affirmations

1. It is human to make mistakes.
2. I can grow and learn from my mistakes.
3. I am compassionate and understanding with myself.
4. I forgive myself for whatever suffering I caused myself or others.
5. I am doing the best I can with the awareness that I have.
6. Write your own affirmation.

Words to Consider

To err is human, to forgive is divine.

—Alfred, Lord Tennyson

Self-Care Activity for Day 13

In your recovery journal, record a past incident for which you have not forgiven yourself. It might be something recent or something that occurred long ago. Start by choosing an experience that is only mild to moderately distressing; deal with the heavy material when you have more practice with this process.

Now ask yourself, "If I could go back in time and *bring my current knowledge and awareness with me*, how would I have handled the situation? How could I have acted differently?" Write your responses in your journal.

Answering these questions helps you understand that you probably *did not* have your current wisdom and knowledge available to you in the past. You made the best choice you could with the limited awareness you possessed.

Letting Go of Shame

Imagine the following situation: You have missed work for a week, and your boss asks you the reason for your absence. Which would you rather say: "I was hospitalized for pneumonia," or "I was too depressed to show up"?

Despite the fact that depression and other mental disorders are largely *organic* conditions whose seat lies in the brain, a societal view still persists that they are the result of weak wills or defects in character. Too often those who suffer from these conditions *internalize* this stigma and feel like something is wrong with them. As one client recently confessed, "I feel like damaged goods."

A powerful way to challenge this untruth is to realize that anyone who must battle a mood disorder is not a wimp, but a strong and courageous individual who has the Herculean task of bearing and transforming intense pain. Wrestling with inner demons is not for the faint of heart. I am reminded of what

Christopher Reeve said about this type of heroism shortly after he became paralyzed:

> When the first Superman movie came out, I was frequently asked, "What is a hero?" My answer was that a hero is someone who commits a courageous action without considering the consequences—a soldier who crawls out of a foxhole to drag an injured buddy to safety. I also meant people who are slightly larger than life: Houdini and Lindbergh, John Wayne, JFK, and Joe DiMaggio. Now my answer is completely different. I think of a hero as an ordinary individual who finds the strength to persevere and endure in spite of overwhelming obstacles.

By Reeve's definition, anybody who ever struggles with crippling depression or a mental health problem is a hero. People need the heroic qualities of courage, endurance, and persistence to overcome these conditions. Thus, rather than see yourself as "defective," think of yourself as a strong and competent person who deals with an imbalanced nervous system. This is the truth of who you are.

Healing Affirmations

1. My struggle is evidence that I am human.
2. I am a normal person responding to a challenging condition.
3. I release the shame and negative self-talk I have about my situation.
4. I accept myself as I am—with my strengths and my struggles.
5. I am a strong and courageous person.
6. Write your own affirmation.

Words to Consider

The best students get the hardest problems.

—Anonymous

Self-Care Activity for Day 14

Today ask yourself if you have "come out" about being in a mental or emotional state that makes it difficult to function. Do you feel safe to tell others about your struggle? If so, who are the people to whom you can speak—a friend, spouse, therapist, and so on? Do you keep your situation hidden from some people? What would happen if these people found out about your struggle?

In addition, ask yourself if you blame yourself for being depressed or anxious. Do you think a weak will or bad attitude causes your condition? Are you ashamed of your situation? Or do you see yourself as a normal person who is dealing with a biochemical imbalance or a very difficult situation (for example, going through a divorce)?

Record the answers to these questions in your recovery journal. If you notice that you carry shame about your condition or situation, share these feelings with someone who understands—such as a therapist or an individual who has experienced a mental disorder.

Bearing the Unbearable Pain

One task you face as a sufferer of depression and other mood disorders is to deal with the intense emotional pain. We cannot describe this pain as stabbing, shooting, or burning; neither can its sensations be localized to any one part of the body. It is an all-encompassing, crucifying pain that slowly permeates every fiber of one's being. On the eve of his hospitalization for suicidal depression, author William Styron said, "I would rather have my arm amputated without anesthesia than to be having the kind of pain I am feeling at this moment."

How does one cope with such intense discomfort? Ironically, fighting against the hurt makes it worse. The more you push against your suffering, the more it intensifies. This principle is delightfully illustrated in the children's book *There's No Such Thing as a Dragon*. The story begins when a young boy named Billy awakens and discovers a small dragon the size of a kitten sitting at the foot of his bed. He wants to keep the dragon as a pet, but his parents refuse to acknowledge that it exists. "There's no such thing as a dragon," they tell Billy. Consequently, the unacknowledged dragon grows larger and larger until it bursts through the roof of the house and runs down the street carrying the house on its back. Only when Billy pets the dragon and says "You are real" does it shrink back to its original size.

This story illustrates an important principle—that when you acknowledge your "inner dragons" (that is, your painful feelings) without trying to judge, change, or resist them in any way, they are more likely to be manageable. In this way, you can learn to cope with the mental and emotional pain. Over a period of time, you can learn to live your life around it. Eventually, the turbulent waters become calm again.

Healing Affirmations

1. I am learning to manage my emotional pain.
2. I ride the wave of my pain.
3. My pain is intense, but it is bearable.
4. With support, I can make it through this ordeal.
5. This, too, shall pass.
6. Write your own affirmation.

Words to Consider

In the midst of winter, I found that there lay
within me an invincible summer.

—*Albert Camus*

Self-Care Activity for Day 15

Today think of your pain or distress as a large approaching wave. As the wave makes contact, see if you can ride the wave by focusing on your breath. Breathe through the sensations by slowly inhaling and exhaling. Don't try to analyze or resist what is happening. Just breathe. This kind of gentle surrender can help you soften around the pain so it decreases in intensity.

A second technique involves monitoring your self-talk. For example, if you find yourself saying, "This pain is unbearable," change it to, "This pain is barely bearable." If you keep telling yourself, "I can't take it," change the words to "I can barely take it." Notice if the pain shifts.

Another technique for tolerating distress is to turn your attention to a pleasant experience from the past. See if reliving a pleasurable memory gives you a temporary break from the pain. You might also visualize yourself lying on a warm, tropical beach or another soothing natural setting.

Record your experiences in your recovery journal.

The Healing Power of
Light and Sound

Which of these images, a bright sunny sky or a dark overcast one, do you imagine that most people feel drawn
to? The positive effect of light on mood seems intuitively obvi-
ous. Adequate exposure to light is necessary for the proper
function of your brain and your sense of well-being. Perhaps
this is why many spiritual paths teach that God and light are
one and the same (for example, think of phrases such as "saved
by the light" and "embraced by the light").

In practical terms, you can benefit from the light by spending time outdoors, especially during the early part of the day.
Walking or running in the early morning is a good way to
do this.

On your walk you may also want to bring along your
Walkman or CD player and listen to your favorite music.
Studies have shown that music can reduce stress and tension,
calm the emotions, still the mind, and restore hope and inspiration. (Think of the soothing, reverential tones of Gregorian

chants or Tibetan bells.) Music can be very relaxing and induce learning, especially when it follows a rhythm of sixty to seventy beats per minute. Or a rousing symphony can be just what you need to feel renewed and energized.

In my recovery program, I make use of music in two ways: In the morning, I play inspiring music (such as Johnny Nash's "I Can See Clearly Now") to motivate me as I ride my stationary bike for a half hour. In the evening I play classical music or a relaxation tape to help me wind down from the day. Here is how one person describes the benefits of music in his life:

> Music is a big help with my mood. I sing with a chorus
> Monday evenings, and it always boosts my energy and
> thoughts. The music continues in my head afterward
> and drives away any negative thoughts I might be
> having.

Light and sound are two natural mood enhancers. May you find fulfilling ways to make them a part of your daily life.

Healing Affirmations

1. I let the heat of the sun penetrate every cell of my body.

2. I envision light cleansing my whole body, bringing healing and strength.

3. I can focus the light that surrounds me into calm, clear thoughts.

4. I feel the sound of music flowing through me, making me vital and creative.

5. The music I listen to relaxes and inspires me.

6. Write your own affirmation.

Words to Consider

Whenever I feel afraid, I whistle a happy tune.

—*Rodgers and Hammerstein,* The King and I

Self-Care Activity for Day 16

Today take inventory about the presence of light in your life. Ask yourself, "Am I getting enough exposure to natural light?"

If the weather permits, go outside and practice feeling the heat of the sun throughout your whole body. Look up toward the sky, and let yourself bathe in the healing light. Even if it is overcast, see if you can appreciate the natural light of the outdoors. Use your other senses, such as touch (for example, feel the breeze on your skin) and smell, to engage yourself with the surrounding environment. If the weather is inclement, you may have to wait for another day.

Second, ask yourself, "What kind of music helps me feel better?" Make a catalog of your favorite musical tunes, noting which ones relax you and which you can use for inspiration. Find time today to listen to one of your favorite pieces of music, noting if any improvements in your mood or physical well-being occur. Feel free to record these changes in your recovery journal.

Day 17

Moving through Grief

A dvances in brain science show that major depression and other mental disorders are genetically and biologically based. Nonetheless, it normally takes an environmental trigger to initiate an episode. One of the most common triggers is loss—specifically the loss of a love. In my practice over two-thirds of the clients who seek help recently experienced a divorce or breakup of a primary relationship. As psychiatrist Thomas Lewis states in his book *A General Theory of Love:*

> Anyone who has grieved a death has known despair from the inside: the leaden inertia of the body, the global indifference to everything but the loss, the aversion to food, the urge to closet oneself away, the inability to sleep, the relentless grayness of the world. Grief can give you some insight into what it is like to have a major depression.

Yet, as described by Sigmund Freud in his famous paper "Mourning and Melancholia," it is not the grief itself, but the lack of completion of grief that leads to problems. Elizabeth Kübler-Ross identified the five stages of grieving a death as denial, anger, bargaining, depression, and acceptance. When we do not fully grieve a serious loss, we can get stuck in the depression phase of the process. This can lead to ongoing low-grade depression (*dysthymia*) or periodic incapacitating depression.

If you sense you only incompletely grieved losses from the past, much exists that you can do in the present. Working with a grief counselor or a therapist can help you to return and perform your mourning. As you go through the process of releasing blocked emotions, you experience a greater vitality in your body and spirit. Because you are not expending extra energy to deaden the pain, you feel more vital and alive.*

Loss does not have to lead to depression. When you get the right kind of support to fully feel your feelings and move through them, the sadness can gradually resolve itself. This is what the psalmist meant when he said, "Those who sow in pain shall reap in joy" (Psalms 126:5).

---

* If you are experiencing an episode of major depression, grieving losses may not be sufficient to ease your symptoms. This is because a physiological imbalance has occurred in your nervous system. Consequently, you may need to seek treatment with a mental health professional.

Healing Affirmations

1. I can get the support I need to feel my grief safely.
2. I can give myself the time I need to grieve fully.
3. I can survive the loss of a love.
4. As I grieve my loss, the intensity of the painful feelings eases.
5. This, too, shall pass.
6. Write your own affirmation.

Words to Consider

Blessed are they that mourn, for they shall be comforted.

—Matthew 5:4

Self-Care Activity for Day 17

Today take inventory of the losses you have experienced in your life. These losses might include death (of a person or pet), a move, a divorce or breakup, a school or business failure, a loss of health, unfulfilled dreams, a lost opportunity, or the losses associated with a traumatic childhood.

Write these down in your recovery journal. Note whatever steps you took to grieve these losses. What has helped and what has not? Do you still feel a sense of incompleteness or lack of resolution regarding any losses? If so, what steps might you take to bring some healing to this experience?

Day 18

The Benefits of Employment

When asked for his definition of mental health, Sigmund Freud replied, "The ability to work and to love." For those of us who suffer from depression and other mental disorders, having a work focus is a crucial part of the recovery process. Employment is therapeutic for a variety of reasons. To begin, work brings structure and a daily routine into your life. Optimal amounts of structure have been shown to decrease the symptoms of anxiety and depression.

In addition, work draws you outside of yourself and brings you into contact with other people, making it less likely that you will ruminate and dwell on your own problems. Work also provides a sense of identity and independence (volunteer work provides many of the same benefits). As one middle-aged woman recently testified at a mental health conference, "The most important factor in my recovery was being able to return to work!" Conversely, a person's lack of employment or being involved in stressful work or work that does not express a genuine passion can worsen mental and emotional problems.

For work to have maximum therapeutic value, it should be meaningful. Such meaning is inherent in the practice of "Right Livelihood," which originated as an aspect of the Buddha's Noble Eightfold Path to Enlightenment. To practice Right Livelihood means finding a way to earn a living in which what you do benefits humans, animals, plants, and the earth—or is at least minimally harmful. Right Livelihood is about expressing your natural talents and gifts in a way that brings you joy, blesses the world, and produces a livable income. It is an expression of your deepest self that does the following:

- provides intrinsic satisfaction ("I do this work because I love doing it.")
- makes serving people and creating something meaningful, beautiful, or useful the *primary* reward; one may still earn a high income, but making money is not the primary motivation
- gives expression to the values that you hold

While finding all of the above qualities in one's work may not always be possible, it is something for which to strive. Clearly, the passion and joy you experience when you find your Right Livelihood are wonderful antidotes to mental suffering as well as being a blessing for the entire planet.

Healing Affirmations

1. Being employed is good for my mental health.
2. I am thankful for the structure and support that my job provides in my life.
3. I feel blessed to be able to provide a service through my job.
4. How I do my work matters much more than what I do.
5. I stay open to work opportunities that come my way.
6. Write your own affirmation.

Words to Consider

Work is love made visible.

–*Kahlil Gibran*, The Prophet

Self-Care Activity for Day 18

Today reflect on the value of work in your life. If you are employed, think about the ways work contributes to your mental health. If aspects of your work are stressful, note those too.

If you are not employed, reflect on how this impacts your mental health. Is employment something you desire? If so, what kind of work might you enjoy?

If you are going to work today, see if you can make the effort to reach out to someone whom you suspect may be struggling. One idea is simply to share that you know what it is like to feel low and that your coworker is not alone in feeling blue.

Day 19

Bringing Pleasure into Your Life

One of the primary symptoms of depression (and some other mood disorders) is the inability to experience pleasure (the clinical term for this is *anhedonia*). When pleasure is absent from your life, the best that you can hope for is a kind of "negative happiness" that results from the temporary absence of distress. In the words of Woody Allen, "Life fluctuates between the horrible and the miserable." When you are in this state of consciousness, it is hard to imagine, let alone remember, ever feeling good.

One way to remedy this situation (especially when your pain is less intense) is to consciously participate in activities that produce pleasure. Such activities release mood-enhancing chemicals in the brain. Therefore, part of your healing involves systematically scheduling pleasurable activities into your life.

To begin the process, ask yourself, "What activities can I think of that *are* enjoyable to me, *used to be* enjoyable, or *might be* enjoyable?" Examples might include eating a good meal, working in the garden, nurturing a pet, spending time with friends, going to a movie, taking a leisurely walk in the park, going sailing, watching a sunset or sunrise, and so on. If you don't feel motivated to do an activity, you might ask another person to join you. Moving through resistance is often easier when you have support. Once you engage in a pleasurable behavior, the resulting good feelings naturally motivate you to repeat the activity. Eventually, it becomes self-reinforcing.

Another way to experience pleasurable feelings is to create "a library of positive memories." Make a list of the happiest moments of your life. Then go back in time and relive them, using your five senses to recreate, in exquisite detail, those positive experiences. Because the brain cannot differentiate between a real or imagined experience, its neurochemicals take on the same mood-enhancing configuration as they did when the original events occurred. When you feel a bit low or need some inspiration, reexperience those past pleasant memories in the present.

Healing Affirmations

1. I am learning to have pleasure in my life.
2. In the midst of my challenges, I can find moments of joy.
3. I take delight in simple pleasures.
4. I can do fun things with other people.
5. I enhance my mood by recalling pleasurable memories.
6. Write your own affirmation.

Words to Consider

The greatest of God's angels is Joy.

She leans over us and gives us the secret of eternity, which is Love.

I used to weep that all did not share.

—Norman Lee

Self-Care Activity for Day 19

The following are some ideas for activities to help you bring more joy and pleasure into your life:

- Go for a walk.
- Share a hug with a loved one.
- Watch a sunset.
- Watch a funny movie.
- Tell a funny joke.
- Listen to music.
- Receive a massage.
- Take a warm bath.
- Sit in a hot tub.
- Play a musical instrument.
- See a special play.
- Spend time in the garden.
- Drive to the beach.
- Swim, float, wade in the water.
- Pet an animal.
- Treat yourself to a nutritious meal.
- Talk to a friend.
- Attend a sports event.
- Create with clay.
- Make a bouquet of flowers.
- Make a collage.
- Draw/paint a picture.
- Go sailing or canoeing.
- Enjoy a hike.
- Hug a tree.
- Go stargazing.
- Play golf or tennis.
- Ride a bike.
- Read a special novel.
- Enjoy a good cup of tea.
- Visit a museum.
- Watch the clouds.
- Go on a camping trip.
- Practice deep breathing.
- Do a gentle stretch.
- Spend time with a friend.
- Attend a concert.
- Write in your journal.
- Go bird-watching.
- Take a vacation.
- Rent a good video.
- Do aerobics/dance.
- Do yoga.
- Think of something for which you are grateful.
- Think of an enjoyable memory.
- Buy yourself a gift.

Read over this list, and pick at least *one activity* to do *today*. (You can also pick one of your own choosing that does not appear on the list.) In addition, record some enjoyable activities in your recovery journal for future reference. Then see if you can participate in one to three of these activities a week. Making a conscious choice to experience pleasure is a powerful way to change your mood and enhance the quality of your life.

Managing Stress through the Relaxation Response

A key component of managing your mood is learning how to deal with stress in your life. This is because stressors such as a personal loss, a financial setback, or an illness can make a blue mood worse.

Here is a brief description of how stress affects the body: Imagine for a moment that you are walking in the woods, and you spot a bear. Your body turns on an automatic survival mechanism known as the "fight-or-flight" response. In seconds your breathing increases, your immune system shuts down, your heart rate and blood pressure skyrocket, and your muscles become tense as you prepare to fight or flee. Once you make it to safety and perceive that the threat has passed, your systems return to normal.

In modern civilization we don't have to worry about fending off bears or other predators; instead, we experience *chronic psychological* and *social stressors*, such as conflicts at work or home, relationship breakups, having a child on drugs, worries about money, and so on. Even though these stressors are not life-threatening, and in some cases may be only imagined (for example, worrying about the future), the body still releases the same powerful hormones that activate the fight-or-flight response. These chemicals (such as cortisol) can adversely impact the brain, making you more prone to anxiety and depression.

Fortunately, you can alter your response to stress. A counterbalancing mechanism in the brain known as the *relaxation response* produces the *opposite* effects of the fight-or-flight response. When your relaxation response activates, your breathing decreases, your heart rate and blood pressure decrease, your mind slows down, your muscles relax, and your immune system works optimally.

Because those of us who suffer from the blues have a thinner cushion of protection from the effects of stress, we must build periods of relaxation into our daily lives. While it can be tempting to use alcohol to relax (or caffeine to focus), you run the risk of developing a new problem if you are prone to addiction—chemical dependency. If you feel stressed, a variety of tools—for example, deep breathing, exercise, massage, hydrotherapy, listening to relaxing music, positive self-talk, prescribed medication, and so on—can help you relax. Today see if you can commit to setting aside fifteen minutes to relax and "just be." Doing this on a regular basis pays huge dividends for your mental and emotional health.

Healing Affirmations

1. I can manage the effects of stress in my life.
2. When I begin to feel stress, I step back and take a deep breath.
3. I take time to breathe deeply every day.
4. When I feel low or anxious, I find someone to talk to.
5. I set aside time to relax and just be.
6. Write your own affirmation.

Words to Consider

Serenity is not the absence of the storm,
but peace amidst the storm.

—*Alcoholics Anonymous*

Self-Care Activity for Day 20

Today practice a simple stress-reduction breathing technique that elicits "the relaxation response." The relaxation response has two primary components:

1. focus of attention
2. passive disregard for thought—you assume the position of the "witness," passively noticing your thoughts without trying to change or control them

To begin, find a quiet place where outside noise is minimal. Pick a place that feels safe and protected. Choose any position in which you feel comfortable. If you sit in a chair, pick one that has good back support. Then proceed as follows:

1. Sit quietly in a comfortable position and close your eyes.
2. Relax your muscles, beginning at the soles of the feet and slowly working up to the face.
3. Breathe in and out through your nose, becoming aware of the rhythm of your breathing. On the out breath, say the word *one* silently to yourself. For example, breathe in and then breathe out, saying the word *one*; breathe in and then breathe out, saying the word *one*; and so on. Breathe easily and naturally.
4. Continue for ten to twenty minutes. You may open your eyes to check the time, but do not use an alarm. When you finish, sit quietly for several minutes, first with your eyes closed and then with your eyes opened. Do not stand up for a few minutes.
5. During the process, maintain a passive attitude, and permit relaxation to occur at its own pace. When you

notice the mind beginning to wander, gently refocus your attention on the word *one* (or whatever word you use as your focus word). Remain the neutral witness and watch the mind without becoming its thoughts.

This type of meditation works best if practiced over a period of time (see if you can commit for a period of five weeks). The best time to practice the relaxation response is when you are undisturbed. Doing it in the morning can set the mood for the day. Try to avoid practicing within two hours of a meal, as digestion seems to interfere with the elicitation of the relaxation response.

Ideally, set aside ten to twenty minutes once or twice a day to do this practice. If you participate regularly, the relaxation response becomes automatic. The more you practice, the more quickly you enter a state of serenity and peace.

Reducing Anxiety

Fear is a natural human emotion. It is normal to feel fear when you are in danger or in an apprehensive situation such as taking a test or awaiting the outcome of a biopsy. But sometimes trauma or a malfunction of body chemistry can activate the fight-or-flight mechanism even when no real threat exists. This kind of clinical anxiety is like being stalked by an imaginary tiger. The feeling of being in danger never goes away.

As with depression, you can use a variety of approaches to decrease anxiety. Because anxiety clearly has physical symptoms, techniques for relaxing the body are a starting point in reducing anxiety. These include abdominal breathing and the relaxation response that you learned in yesterday's lesson. Regular exercise can also significantly reduce anxiety. Exercise decreases skeletal muscle tension, breaks down arousal-producing chemicals in the bloodstream, and discharges pent-up frustration and anger.

Monitoring your self-talk is another important way to reduce anxiety. Worrisome thoughts and fearful self-talk can produce anxious feelings. An example is the thought "What if

I have an accident while I'm driving home?" Replace such negative self-talk with positive counterstatements, such as "I am a safe driver," or "I can feel some tension in my body and still drive safely."

You can also reduce anxiety by making changes in your diet. Stimulants such as caffeine and nicotine can make you more prone to anxiety and panic attacks. Other dietary substances such as sugar and certain food additives, as well as food sensitivities, can make some people feel anxious. Seeing a nutritionally oriented physician or therapist may help you identify and eliminate possible offending substances from your diet. Prescription medications (Xanax, Ativan, Klonopin, and so on) can also treat the symptoms of anxiety. Because these medications are habit-forming, they should be used short-term in conjunction with the other tools we have mentioned.*

Finally, staying focused in the present can reduce many anxious feelings that arise from worrying about the future. The phrase "Right here, right now, I'm okay" affirms your safety in response to worries about what might occur. Many fears about the future boil down to a single fear—*the fear of not being able to cope*. Affirmations such as "I can handle it," "I will draw to myself the support I need," or "God is watching over me" help you trust that things will work out.

---

* If you suffer from a serious anxiety disorder, you may want to locate a clinic in your area that *specializes* in the treatment of anxiety. Your local hospital or mental health clinic can give you a referral. In addition, you may wish to call (800) 64-PANIC to receive helpful material from the National Institute of Mental Health.

Healing Affirmations

1. I have tools to manage my anxiety.
2. With these tools, I can handle what comes my way.
3. At the first signs of anxiety, I take steps to deal with the situation.
4. When I feel anxious, I find someone to talk to.
5. I have the courage to move through my fears.
6. Write your own affirmation.

Words to Consider

I had a great many problems,
but most of them never happened to me.

—Mark Twain

Self-Care Activity for Day 21

Today choose either or both of the following activities:

- Pick a situation in your life that brings up anxiety for you. This can range from fear of public speaking, leaving the house, or asking someone for help. Record in your recovery journal any negative or fearful self-talk that arises when you think about the event. Then ask yourself, "Are these beliefs accurate? Do they reflect the truth of the situation?" Someone waiting to be interviewed for a job might think, "I'm sure I'll blow it." This is called fortune-telling or catastrophizing. At this point, the person can challenge that assumption and replace it with a more supportive and realistic statement—for example, "I have prepared for this interview. I will relax and do my best."
- A second exercise is to monitor your emotional state during the day, noting any moments during which you begin to feel anxious. See if you can detect the first signs of anxiety. Where do you notice it in your body— in your stomach, in your heart, or with your breathing? What thoughts are you thinking? Do you see a causal relationship between your thinking and the anxiety?

Can you change your thoughts to a more positive frame? When you do, what happens?

Write down your observations in your recovery journal.

He Who Laughs Lasts

The proverb "Laughter is good medicine" is more than just a saying. Ever since Norman Cousins published his memoir *Anatomy of an Illness*, in which he describes how he healed himself of a fatal illness through vitamin C and laughter, the medical world has come to recognize the therapeutic value of humor. A belly laugh, said Cousins, is equivalent to "an internal jogging." It enhances respiration and circulation, oxygenates the blood, decreases stress hormones in the brain, and prevents "hardening of the attitudes."

Have you ever had a depressing thought in the middle of a good laugh? It's next to impossible. When you laugh, your brain produces natural mood elevators that free you from your attachment to pain and suffering. Laughter also helps you keep your life in its proper perspective. When you laugh at yourself, you take yourself far less seriously. As the saying tells us, "Angels can fly because they take themselves so lightly."

In one example of the therapeutic value of laughter, an elderly man was admitted to a hospital suffering from severe depression, having not eaten or spoken for several days. Shortly afterward, a clown entered his room. In thirty minutes the patient was laughing, eating, and talking.

If it has been a while since you had a good laugh, let your child come out and play. Laughter offers a powerful distraction from both physical and emotional pain. It can bring the return of joy and peace. Best of all, laughter is free and has no negative side effects.

Healing Affirmations

1. Laughter is good medicine.
2. I let myself laugh and see the light side of life.
3. I practice my sense of humor.
4. I seek out people who have a good sense of humor.
5. I can buoy my mood by recalling a very funny, special moment.
6. Write your own affirmation.

Words to Consider

A cheerful heart is a good medicine.

—Proverbs 17:22

Self-Care Activity for Day 22

Today make a list in your recovery journal of the ways you can build laughter into your daily life. Examples include having a humorous poster in your home or at the office, reading your favorite comic strip, telling jokes with your friends, receiving jokes over the Internet, reading a book of humor, or watching videos of your favorite comedians.

After you create your list, pick one of the activities and do it today (or as soon as you can). This might be the perfect time to rent that comedy you have wanted to see for years.

The Power of Self-Esteem

Self-esteem is a powerful ally for healing from the blues. When you truly value yourself and feel you are worthwhile, you are much more likely to engage in self-nurturing strategies that help you get well and stay well. A person with healthy self-esteem says, "Because I am of value, I deserve to feel better. I am committed to doing whatever it takes to bring about my recovery."

Unfortunately, people who suffer from depression and other mood disorders find that their self-esteem plummets like stocks in a bear market. As television journalist Mike Wallace said about his own depression, "I felt lower than a snake's belly. I thought the world would be better off without me." Comparing yourself to other people compounds such feelings of failure. We do this in a variety of ways—by focusing on how others make more money, are better looking, go to a better school, and so on. For example, my self-esteem took a beating when my depressive disorder forced me to drop out of the workforce for ten months.

Here is how my therapist responded to my belief that my lack of employment made me a "nobody": "Douglas," she said, "who you are is not a function of how much money you make. Who you are is not a function of how many credentials you have. Who you are is not a function of your vocational identity or occupational title."

Pat continued, "Your friends may work on the twenty-second floor of an office building, but your 'work' right now is to heal from this illness, a much harder job than being a vice president of U.S. Bank."

"How do you figure that?" I asked.

"Just managing to stay functional, given your level of pain, is a major achievement. I'm sorry that no one is giving you stock options for your display of courage. But the absence of financial reward does not invalidate the important work you are doing."

As Pat's feedback made clear, even if you suffer from a mental disorder, you can learn to let go of "the weapon of comparison" and see that your essential goodness depends not on what you do, but on your essential worthiness. Hold to this truth. No matter what has happened to you or will happen, you will never lose your essential value. You are special.

Healing Affirmations

1. I am a valuable person.
2. I take responsibility for my well-being.
3. No one exists who is exactly like me. I have my own unique gifts to offer the world.
4. I release the need to compare myself to others.
5. I see myself as a work in progress, growing and evolving.
6. Write your own affirmation.

Words to Consider

A man cannot be comfortable without his own approval.

—Mark Twain

Self-Care Activity for Day 23

Today approach a person in your life whom you know and trust. Ask that person to share with you one or more qualities they appreciate about you. Allow yourself to take this information in without analyzing or judging it. Then write these traits down in your recovery journal.

Afterward turn these into positive affirmations. For example, if your friend told you that you were kind, write the affirmation "I am kind," or "I am a kind and supportive person." Repeating these statements helps you strengthen your self-esteem. Also say these affirmations when you feel low or unworthy.

Accepting Change

O ne of the most important attributes for mental health is flexibility—the ability to adapt oneself to life and to change. In our quest for safety and security, we like to see things as solid and stable. We become attached to things continuing as they are. Yet the physical world is more fluid than we realize, and the only constant in the universe is change. The following parable can help remind us of this truth:

> According to an ancient tale, a group of warriors attacked and captured a Sufi village. The king of the victorious tribe called the Sufi leaders and said that unless they fulfilled his wish, he would put the entire village to death the following morning. The king's wish was to know the secret of what would make him happy when he was sad and sad when he was happy.
>
> The village people constructed a large bonfire, and all night long their wise men and women strove to answer the riddle: what makes a person happy when he or she is sad and sad when he or she is happy? Finally, sunrise came and the king entered the village.

Approaching the wise ones, he asked, "Have you fulfilled my request?" "Yes!" they replied. The king was delighted. "Well, show me your gift." One of the wise men then reached into a pouch and presented the king with a gold ring. The king was perplexed. "I have no need of more gold," he exclaimed. "How can this ring make me happy when I am sad and sad when I am happy?" Then the king looked again, and this time he saw an inscription: it read "This, too, shall pass."

Understanding that nothing lasts forever can give you the flexibility to "go with the flow" and avoid the clinging that leads to suffering. In this way, you learn to accept both the good and bad times equally, understanding that all of life's teachings are necessary for your spiritual growth. With this realization, you will be like the great saint who proclaimed, "One to me is loss and gain, one to me is pleasure and pain, one to me is fame and shame."

Healing Affirmations

1. I am open to change.
2. Like a willow in the wind, I can be flexible.
3. Shift happens.
4. I have faith in my resilience.
5. Rather than seeking pleasure and avoiding pain, I accept both as having equal benefit.
6. Write your own affirmation.

Words to Consider

Remember, no human condition is ever permanent;
then you will not be overjoyed in good fortune
nor too sorrowful in misfortune.

—Socrates

Hang on tightly; let go lightly.

—Ram Dass

Self-Care Activity for Day 24

The principle of impermanence is a central teaching of Buddhist philosophy. To understand the nature of this truth, look back at your life five years ago. Ask yourself, "Are things the same as they once were, or have any changes occurred during these time periods?" Note or write down any shifts that occurred in the areas of health, relationships, work, finances, physical location, and so on.

As you take inventory of your experiences, you will see that many things you once thought of as fixed and stable have now changed.

Another exercise is to pick a time in your life when you experienced great change. What was your attitude toward the situation? Do you remember fighting against the change or flowing with it?

Now think of another time when you were maybe able to accept the change. How was your experience different?

Don't Give Up Five Minutes
before the Miracle

Yesterday you learned the important truth that the only constant in the universe is change. Understanding the principle of impermanence (that is, "This, too, shall pass") can be lifesaving when you encounter the feeling of hopelessness that is one of the most common symptoms of depression and other mood disorders.

When we lose hope, we think, "Not only am I experiencing this horrible pain, but it is here forever. I am permanently frozen in this hellish state. I am trapped in a tunnel with both entrances sealed off and a sign that reads 'No Exit'!"

If you find yourself in such a state of despair, try to realize that your brain is playing a nasty trick on you. You are not really stuck; you just feel you are. A chemical imbalance in your brain cells prevents you from envisioning a positive future. If you fear no way out exists, let the words on the following page console you.

What Goes Down Must Come Up

There can be no death without rebirth.

Every ending is followed by a beginning.

The experience of hell is a precursor to the glory
of heaven.

The ancient phoenix bird was consumed in its own ashes
only to rise again. Christ was crucified only to be resurrected.
The process of death and rebirth is universal.

Yes, you are in pain. At times the feelings of despair may
be so great that you feel you can no longer continue. Nevertheless, the prescription is simple: hang in there!

If you are on the edge of the abyss, don't jump.

If you are going through hell, don't stop.

As long as you are breathing, there is hope.

As long as day follows night, there is hope.

Nothing stays the same forever.

Set an intention to heal, reach out for support,

And you will find help.

Since all things must pass, time is on your side. You may
not know exactly when the change will occur, but I can assure
you that it will. Take one day at a time. At some point, you will
find a way to rise out of your ashes and spread your wings like
a soaring eagle. The joy that awaits you is far greater than the
pain you are experiencing.

Don't give up five minutes before the miracle!

Healing Affirmations

1. What goes down must come up; I know this to be true in my life.

2. I make room for the *possibility* that some unexpected good might grace my life.

3. I can sense the light at the end of the tunnel.

4. I have faith that a benevolent universe will come to support me.

5. This, too, shall pass.

6. Write your own affirmation.

Words to Consider

Never are we nearer the Light
than when the darkness is deepest.

—*Vivekananda*

It is not having been in the dark house;
it is having left it that counts.

—*Teddy Roosevelt*

When going through hell, "Don't stop!"

—*Rev. Tom Costas*

Self-Care Activity for Day 25

When I experienced my most recent depressive episodes, I asked my social worker if I would ever get better.

"What happened with your previous two depressions?" she asked.

"I eventually came out of them," I replied.

"You have your answer then," she responded. "I find that past experience is the best predictor of the future. You will get well now, just as you did in the past."

My social worker's logic gave me hope that my ordeal would eventually come to an end. Apply this principle to your own situation. Think of a time in your life when you experienced a "dark night of the soul." The struggle may have involved your mental health, physical health, work, finances, relationships, and so on. Whatever the situation, ask yourself, "What was my experience during this distressing time? Did I sometimes wonder if I would ever make it to the other side? How did I eventually come out of it?"

By reviewing a number of such experiences, you may come to understand the cyclic and transitory nature of all phenomena—including difficult times. Such an understanding may help you more effectively deal with a *current* crisis by realizing that great truth, "This, too, shall pass."

Day 26

You Have the Power

A classic symptom of depression (and other mood disorders) is the feeling of helplessness—that you cannot change your life for the better. Much of this helplessness arises from the fact that external situations over which you have no control create many of your symptoms of depression and anxiety. For example, some of us were born with a temperament that is more fearful, pessimistic, and withdrawn than other people. Others of us suffered childhood trauma that adversely impacts our brain chemistry and nervous system. Or we may have learned habits of negative thinking through our upbringing and conditioning (for example, a parent who worries a lot inadvertently teaches his or her child to worry too).

In his landmark book *Helplessness*, psychologist Martin Seligman found that when people feel they have no choices or options, they become depressed. He called this phenomenon "learned helplessness." Yet, if you can learn attitudes of helplessness, you can also unlearn them. You can learn new tools and take small steps to impact your life positively. Even when you cannot control your outer circumstances, you can choose how you respond to them. Concentration camp survivor Victor Frankl called this ability to choose one's attitude in any given set of circumstances "the last of the human freedoms."

Therefore, no matter how much the past has adversely affected you, right now you can choose to see yourself as the shaper of your life. The past is not the future. You can learn new and functional coping strategies. Once you grasp the reality that your thoughts and actions make a difference in your life and in the lives of those around you, your healing process can move forward.

Healing Affirmations

1. I have the ability to create support for myself in my life.
2. I assume responsibility for my attitude and my actions.
3. I am taking small, meaningful steps to help myself.
4. I am becoming the director of my life.
5. Feeling empowered greatly enhances my sense of well-being.
6. Write your own affirmation.

Words to Consider

It matters not how straight the gate,
How charged with punishments the scroll,
I am the captain of my fate,
I am the master of my soul.

—William Ernest Henley

Self-Care Activity for Day 26

Have you ever answered "I don't know" or "No" when friends ask if they could do anything to help you? Have you ever said "Whatever" when negotiating with a partner? Have you catastrophized about your current situation, saying, "I will never get out of this pit"? All these responses have their origin in a feeling of helplessness.

Today notice the times when you fall into such an attitude of helplessness. When you do, recognize that this a choice and not an absolute reality. You may *feel* helpless, but you do have choices and options. Ask yourself, "Can I look at this situation in a different light? Are other options available? Even if I can't change my situation, can I change my attitude?"

For example, a client struggling with depression felt stuck in a dead-end accounting job. The feeling of having no options made his depression worse. Then he decided to call the local university and inquire about going back to school to get a degree in art therapy. Simply making the call and learning about the program raised his spirits. Having hope that he could find a more fulfilling way to make a living reduced his depression and made his current job more tolerable.

Finding Purpose and Meaning

ॐ

Social scientists have long observed that rates of depression decrease during wartime and rise during peacetime. This is because during war, people have a clear sense of focus and mission—that is, achieving military victory. This phenomenon demonstrates the importance of having purpose and meaning in your life. During his concentration camp experience, psychiatrist Victor Frankl discovered that if a prisoner had a purpose for living after the war, he was more likely to survive. For some people, that purpose was about reuniting with a loved one; for others, it was about completing a scientific experiment or a work of art; for others, it was about coming home to raise a child.

After the war Frankl realized that the need for meaning was not just applicable to prisoners of war; it was a universal human need. In his role as a psychiatrist, Frankl discovered that many types of mental illness improved when a person found a worthwhile purpose on which to base his or her life. Conversely, he saw many people succumb to depression and other mental disorders when they felt they had "nothing to live for."

When you have an overriding purpose in life—something for which to live greater than yourself—your symptoms, though distressing, become more bearable. You can tolerate the pain, because you focus on an ideal that nurtures and strengthens your spirit.

What do you do when depression robs your life of a sense of meaning? If you feel down or distressed and think you have no purpose, know that your mission is to stay alive until you emerge from the darkness. At that time the meaning and purpose of your life will reappear. Have faith that you have unique gifts to offer.

Healing Affirmations

1. I am open to the idea that my life has purpose and meaning.
2. I strive for an ideal that gives meaning to my life.
3. I give myself over to a purpose greater than myself.
4. I trust that a specific and fulfilling task exists for me.
5. I have a unique place in this world that no one else can duplicate. It is important that I be here.
6. Write your own affirmation.

Words to Consider

Man can bear any how if he has a "why."

—Nietzsche

Self-Care Activity for Day 27

Ask yourself what gives meaning to your life. Here is a simple way to get in touch with your priorities. Imagine that you have an incurable illness and have six months to live. As the doctors inform you of their findings, say to yourself, *"I am going to spend the last months of my life living to the fullest, doing those things that are truly important to me."* Then imagine yourself living out those six months.

Write in your journal what you did, who you saw, and where you went. What do these answers say about what is really important to you? Are you living your values and priorities today?

Some people report that they would continue to live exactly as they do now if they had six months to live. If what gives your life purpose and meaning is already in your life, celebrate it. If you got in touch with a dream that was buried or forgotten, start to imagine how to bring that into your life. Are there concrete steps you can take? The positive actions you take will pay off in greater serenity and improved mental health.

Persistence

Consider these words of Calvin Coolidge: "Nothing in the world can take the place of persistence. Talent will not; nothing is more common than unsuccessful men with talent. Genius will not; unrewarded genius is almost a proverb. Education will not; the world is filled with educated derelicts. Persistence and determination are alone omnipotent. 'Press on!' has been and always will be the answer to every human problem."

Coolidge was right. In the successful pursuit of a vision, persistence always makes the difference. Thomas Edison made over two thousand attempts before he invented the lightbulb. Abraham Lincoln failed in two businesses and lost five elections before he became president.

How does this principle apply to those of us who suffer from anxiety, depression, and other mental disorders? Clearly, the ability to persevere in the face of adversity is an essential part of recovering from emotional disorders. The path to health is rarely straightforward. It may take weeks or months before you can find an effective medication. You may endure minor and major relapses before you reach a place of stability and harmony. It takes patience and faith to hang in there until the right combination of factors turns the tide.

Such patience and perseverance are much easier to cultivate if you belong to a healing community. When others are on the journey with you—family, friends, doctors, therapists, or members of a support group—they can hold the faith and "keep the high watch" when you cannot. During times when your individual willpower is not sufficient to overcome the pain, the combined perseverance of two or more people can make the difference. As the adage from Alcoholics Anonymous states, "Let this circle represent that we can do together that which we cannot do alone."

Healing Affirmations

1. I will make it through this difficult cycle in my life.
2. I will endure.
3. I am developing the resources I need to cope with the challenge before me.
4. With the support of others, I can make it through this time.
5. I am being polished by the windstorms of life.
6. Write your own affirmation.

Words to Consider

A hero is an ordinary individual who finds the strength to persevere and endure in spite of overwhelming obstacles.

—Christopher Reeve

Our greatest glory is not in never falling,
But in rising every time we fall.

—Buddha

Self-Care Activity for Day 28

Today think of someone who persisted and overcame great odds. This can be someone you know personally or someone in the public eye (my favorite is Helen Keller). Imagine yourself walking beside this person and drawing strength and inspiration from him or her. When you need some extra strength or perseverance, call on this image and feeling.

Day 29

Breaking Down to Break Through

One of the scariest aspects of having a mental disorder is having your symptoms become so severe that you become completely incapacitated. Such a collapse was once called a "nervous breakdown." As painful as such an experience can be, it is helpful to realize that having a breakdown can be a precursor to a "breakthrough."

In physics, a phenomenon called the theory of dissipative structures supports this idea. The theory states that "open systems" (those systems having a continuous interchange with the environment) occasionally experience periods of instability. When this imbalance exceeds a certain limit, the system breaks down and enters a state of "creative chaos." Yet, out of chaos and disorganization, a new and higher order spontaneously emerges.*

I believe that what holds true on the physical plane is also valid on the psychological plane. Hence, we can see so-called nervous breakdowns as rites of passage into a more mature

---

* Czech physical chemist Ilya Prigogine won the Nobel Prize in 1977 for identifying this phenomenon.

spiritual consciousness. Researcher Julius Siegal describes it as follows:

> In a remarkable number of cases, those who have suffered and prevail find that after their ordeal, they begin to operate at a higher level than ever before. The terrible experiences of our lives, despite the pain they bring, may become our redemption.

I would never want to trivialize the suffering that mood disorders bring. Nonetheless, I do feel changed for the better having undergone episodes of clinical depression. All that I lost has been restored in a new and better way. Out of the ashes of my old life, a new life has been resurrected.

Hopefully, during times of distress, you can take comfort in realizing that today's death is tomorrow's resurrection. Or, as Paul the apostle said in the book of Romans (8:18), "I consider that the sufferings of the present time are not worthy to be compared with the glory that shall be revealed in us."

Healing Affirmations

1. I take solace in the belief that this painful time is a part of a "birth" process.
2. I can ask people for help as I go through this trying time.
3. I let go of what no longer serves me.
4. I allow myself to be tempered in this fire.
5. I let go and let God.
6. Write your own affirmation.

Words to Consider

The depth of darkness to which you can descend and still live is an exact measure of the height to which you can aspire to reach.

—Laurens van der Post

Enlightenment begins on the other side of despair.

—Jean-Paul Sartre

Self-Care Activity for Day 29

Choose two or three people whom you know or about whom you have read who experienced a "dark night of the soul." Can you see how these experiences might make these people stronger, kinder, wiser, or more compassionate? Have any of these people taken their experiences and created something positive from them? Can you envision anything positive that has come or might come of your own struggle?

Day 30

Relapse Prevention

A s anyone who has experienced a mood disorder knows, recovery is not like getting over the measles—one does not develop an immunity to the disease. Although you can control the symptoms of a mental disorder, the underlying predisposition does not go away. Once you succeed in managing your symptoms, you need to have at your disposal a series of strategies to prevent a major relapse.

This relapse prevention process consists of two stages: In stage one identify the early warning signs that indicate that you may be slipping back into old patterns of distress. In the second stage, respond to symptoms before they get out of hand.

For example, one of my early warning signs of impending depression is insomnia. When depression starts to creep up on me, I wake up at four in the morning and have obsessive thoughts. If this pattern lasts more than a few days, I know I must take action. I increase my exercise level, take a warm bath before bed, and take a small dose of an antidepressant used for sleep. This intervention normally eliminates my sleep disruptions. In addition, if an external stressor triggers the symptoms (for example, difficulties at work), I seek to deal with it appropriately.

In a similar manner, as you learn more about your own mood disorder, you can become aware of your own warning signs and symptoms. Then when they appear, you can be proactive and nip the symptoms in the bud.

Relapse prevention offers great hope that you can manage the symptoms of depression, anxiety, and other mood disorders. Although these conditions are with you, they do not have to control you. You can learn to live with a mental disorder, just as others learn to live with medical conditions such as hypertension and diabetes. Knowing that you have tools and skills to help you manage your symptoms can be a source of peace and comfort.

Healing Affirmations

1. I can learn to recognize my early warning signs of relapse.

2. When symptoms appear, I take action to reduce them.

3. I ask for help when I need it.

4. I feel empowered, knowing I have skills to take care of myself.

5. I have faith that I can cope with whatever arises.

6. Write your own affirmation.

Words to Consider

An ounce of prevention is worth a pound of cure.

—Proverb

Self-Care Activity for Day 30

Today start creating your own "personalized relapse prevention plan." This plan will help you identify and respond to
your personal warning signs of relapse. It will also help you
specify actions you can take once you become aware of those
warning signs.

The following questions are designed to help you build
your relapse prevention plan. Take as much time as you need
to answer them (a few days, a week, a month, and so on).
Write your answers down on a separate page in your recovery
journal with the heading "My Relapse Prevention Plan." You
may want to show your answers to someone on your support
team—your counselor, therapist, prescriber, coach, friend,
family member, and so on.

If you use this book on a month-to-month basis, so that
you recycle through the lessons, review your relapse prevention plan every thirty days, and revise it as your situation
changes. Good luck.

- What warnings indicate that I am becoming depressed
  or anxious or having other symptoms of my disorder?
  (You may want to review what led up to any previous
  episodes to answer this question.)
- When I notice these warning signs, what actions might
  I take to help me cope?
- Whom can I call or talk with to get support? With
  whom will I share my relapse warning signs? Please list

(if you can) three or more people in your relapse
prevention plan.

- Sometimes others spot relapse warning signs in me
  before I do. Do I trust anybody whom I can ask to let
  me know if I am in danger of relapse?
- What are my personal "triggers"—those thoughts,
  events, or situations that can initiate symptoms of my
  mood disorder?
- What steps can I take to reduce the chance of becoming off center in those situations?
- Is it possible to avoid such triggers altogether? How
  might I do so?
- Could I make any changes in my daily activities that
  would reduce the risk of relapse?

The Joy of Service

❧

A fundamental symptom of depression and other mental problems is the tendency to becoming overly focused on one's own suffering. Like the constant throbbing of an abscessed tooth, the emotional pain you suffer can become all encompassing. A practical way to help alleviate this condition is through serving others. Service allows you to transcend your suffering by shifting focus away from yourself. As author Tracy Thompson writes regarding her own recovery from depression, "Help others. Be of service. Only in this way will you find your way out of the prison of self." In this vein, an article in *Psychology Today* reports that volunteer work leads to a phenomenon called "helper's high"—a physiological change in the body that produces physical and emotional well-being, as well as relief from stress-related disorders.

An intriguing example of the therapeutic value of service occurred in the life of Mary Todd Lincoln, who, like her husband President Lincoln, battled depression throughout her life. In the midst of the Civil War, Mary experienced a second depressive breakdown, triggered by the loss of her favorite son and the absence of her husband, who was preoccupied with wartime activities. Shortly after her boy's death, Mary began to volunteer as a nurse's aide in Civil War hospitals. Although the drop of a book at home would have set off a panic attack, Mary was able to stay calm amidst the sounds and shrieks of the tormented patients. By taking the focus off herself through serving others, she transcended her fears.

In thinking about how you are of service, remember that a balance exists between giving and receiving. It is possible to focus so much on others that your own self-care will suffer. The gospels tell us, "Love your neighbor as yourself." In other words, the caring of others is founded on a healthy care of self.

Healing Affirmations

1. Today I give myself in loving service.
2. My suffering gives me compassion for others.
3. As I reach out to others, my own pain decreases.
4. The more I give, the more I receive.
5. I allow myself to feel the joy of giving.
6. Write your own affirmation.

Words to Consider

It is one of the most beautiful compensations of
this life that no man can sincerely try to help
another without helping himself.

—Ralph Waldo Emerson

The prevailing question of the day is,
"What have you done for others?"

—Martin Luther King Jr.

Self-Care Activity for Day 31

Today make a list of those areas in which you are being of service or in which you might be of service. Many arenas exist in which this can occur—through family life, in one's job or career, through volunteer work, contributing to charities, mentoring young people, working with the dying, helping someone in need, and so on.

The amount of service that you perform does not have to be large. If you feel limited in your capacity to give, start with some form of service that requires a low level of commitment—such as nurturing a pet or a plant. Extending yourself even a little bit will be good for the recipient and good for you. As Aesop tells us in his parable of the lion and the mouse, "No act of kindness, however small, is ever wasted."

Appendix A

Am I Okay?:
An Overview of Mental
and Emotional Disorders

∽✞∾

The first step in becoming liberated from depression and other mood disorders is to recognize and understand the nature of the condition. Getting proper help begins with proper diagnosis. The purpose of the following pages is to provide a clear understanding of the signs and symptoms of the major mood disorders so you can determine if you or a loved one need to seek treatment.

The disorders we will cover include clinical depression, manic-depressive illness (bipolar disorder), dysthymia, cyclothymia, postpartum depression, seasonal affective disorder (SAD), generalized anxiety disorder, panic disorder, agoraphobia, social phobia (social anxiety disorder), post-traumatic stress disorder (PTSD), and substance disorders.

Clinical Depression

A depressive illness is a "whole body" disorder, involving one's physiology, biochemistry, mood, thoughts, and behavior. It affects the way you eat and sleep and the way you think and feel about yourself, others, and the world. Clinical depression is not a passing blue mood or a sign of personal weakness.

Subtle changes in the brain's chemistry can create a terrible malaise in the body/mind/spirit that affects every dimension of your being.

As we enter the twenty-first century, the rising incidence of depression is particularly notable. Depression is now the second most disabling condition in the United States (surpassed only by heart disease) and the fourth most disabling worldwide. The disorder does not discriminate among its victims—it affects all age groups, all economic groups, and all gender and ethnic categories. While the average age of onset was once a person's midthirties, it is now moving toward adolescence and even early childhood. At any given moment, somewhere between fifteen and twenty million Americans suffer from depressive disorders, and about one in five will develop the illness at some point during their lifetimes.

Depression is a complex disorder, and its symptoms express themselves on many levels. Depression creates physical problems, behavioral problems, distorted thinking, changes in emotional well-being, troubled relationships, and spiritual emptiness. We can divide the symptoms of major depression into three categories:

1. Disturbances of emotion and mood
2. Changes in the "housekeeping" functions of the brain—those that regulate sleep, appetite, energy, and sexual function
3. Disturbances of thinking and concentration

The most common symptoms of clinical depression include the following:

- chronically sad or empty mood
- loss of interest in ordinary pleasurable activities, including sex
- decreased energy, fatigue, feeling slowed down, slowed movement, and slurred speech
- sleep disturbances (insomnia, early morning waking, or oversleeping)
- eating disturbances (loss of appetite, significant weight loss or weight gain)
- difficulty concentrating, impaired memory, difficulty in making decisions
- agitated actions (pacing, hand-wringing, and so on)
- feelings of guilt, worthlessness, or helplessness
- feelings of hopelessness and despair
- thoughts and/or talk of death and suicide
- irritability or excessive crying
- social withdrawal or isolation
- chronic aches and pains that don't respond to treatment
- suicide attempts
- increase in addictive behavior

In the workplace, you can recognize depression by the following symptoms:

- morale problems/lack of cooperation
- difficulty concentrating
- safety problems, accidents, listlessness

- absenteeism
- frequent complaints of being tired all the time
- complaints of unexplained aches and pains
- alcohol or drug abuse
- blaming others
- increased complaints about a spouse or significant other

For those at home, these symptoms may appear as follows:

- a lack of interest in daily self-care routines
- less attention paid to children (dependents)
- not wanting to go out of the house
- not finding any meaning to one's day
- increased addictive behavior kept a secret
- feeling overwhelmed by ordinary tasks
- feelings of guilt and worthlessness

To best apply this cluster of symptoms to your own situation, think of your symptoms in terms of three categories—*number*, *duration*, and *intensity*.

1. Number. The symptoms of depression are "additive"—that is, the greater the number of symptoms you have, the more likely that you are clinically depressed. According to the *Diagnostic and Statistical Manual of Mental Disorders* (DSM-IV), a person should have five or more of these symptoms to consider him- or herself "clinically depressed."

2. Duration. The longer you are down in the dumps, the more likely it is that you are clinically depressed. According to the DSM-IV, the five or more symptoms must exist for at least *two weeks* for a diagnosis of major depression to be made. (In the case of dysthymia or chronic low-grade depression, symptoms must be present for *two years* or more.)

3. Intensity. Many of us can feel emotional pain and still cope with our daily existence. Some experiences of depression fall within the normal course of living. The pain of major depression can be so great, however, that its intensity (along with the number and duration of symptoms) can significantly impair one's ability to cope.

Getting proper help for depression begins with proper diagnosis. The questionnaire that follows may help you determine if you suffer from depression.

Self-Rating Scale for Depression

Have either of the following symptoms been present nearly every day *for at least two weeks?*

A. Have you been sad, blue, or "down in the dumps"?

B. Have you lost interest or pleasure in all or almost all the things you usually do (work, hobbies, or interpersonal relationships)?

If either A or B is true, continue. If not, you probably do not have a depressive illness. Now continue by answering the following statements:

- Have any of the following symptoms been present nearly every day *for at least two weeks?*

1. A poor appetite or overeating?	No	Yes
2. Insomnia—trouble falling asleep or night-time awakenings?	No	Yes

3. Oversleeping (going to bed a lot earlier than usual, staying in bed later than usual, or taking long naps)?   No   Yes

4. Do you have low energy, chronic fatigue, or do you feel slowed down?   No   Yes

5. Are you less active or talkative than usual?   No   Yes

6. Do you feel restless or agitated?   No   Yes

7. Do you avoid the company of other people more than you used to?   No   Yes

8. Have you lost interest or enjoyment in pleasurable activities, including sex?   No   Yes

9. Do you fail to experience pleasure when positive things occur—such as being praised, being given presents, and so on?   No   Yes

10. Do you have feelings of inadequacy or decreased feelings of self-esteem, or are you overly or increasingly self-critical?   No   Yes

11. Are you less efficient, or do you accomplish less at school, work, or home?   No   Yes

12. Do you feel less able to cope with the routine responsibilities of daily life?   No   Yes

13. Do you find that your concentration is poor and you have difficulty making decisions (even trivial ones)?   No   Yes

14. Do you think and/or talk about death and suicide?   No   Yes

15. Have you at any time in the past acted unusually happy for more than two weeks?   No   Yes

If A or B is true and if you answered yes to five or more of the above questions, you may have a major depressive illness. If you answered yes to number 15, you may consider whether major depression is but one phase of a bipolar disorder.

For the diagnosis to be complete, however, you should have a complete physical exam and blood workup to rule out other medical problems such as anemia, reactive hypoglycemia, and low thyroid, all of which cause symptoms that may mimic those of major depression. Specifically, you want a test of the thyroid function called the TSH (thyroid stimulating hormone) stimulation test as well as the TRH (thyrotropin releasing hormone) stimulation test. (The TRH test is complicated to perform and, thus, doctors rarely order it; however, it can pick up on thyroid disorders that the TSH test cannot.)

Manic-Depressive Illness (Bipolar Disorder)

Terror drove me from place to place. My breath failed me as I pictured my brain paralyzed. Ah, Clara, no one knows the suffering, the sickness, the despair of this illness, except those so crushed.

—Composer Robert Schumann, speaking of his manic depression

Although manic-depressive illness (which affects two to three million people) is less common than major depression, it maintains a high profile because of the many creative artists who suffered from it. Examples include Edgar Allen Poe, Tennessee Williams, Ezra Pound, Virginia Woolfe, Vincent van Gogh,

Alfred Tennyson, Cole Porter, and Robert Schumann. In recent times, celebrities such as Abbie Hoffman, columnist Art Buchwald, actress Patty Duke, actress Margot Kidder, and CNN's Ted Turner have been similarly afflicted.

Manic depression has two distinct sides—the *depressive* state and the *manic* state. Mania is a seemingly heavenly state of mind in which all the world is beautiful and everything seems possible. The following are some of the most common characteristics of mania:

- optimism
- impulsivity
- euphoria
- spending large amounts of money
- little need for sleep
- socially inappropriate behavior
- little need for food
- heightened sense of awareness
- irritability
- flight of ideas
- inflated self-concept
- racing thoughts
- grandiose schemes
- pressured speech
- unrealistic thinking
- tremendous energy
- poor judgment
- enhanced creativity

- loss of inhibition
- hyperactivity
- delusional thinking
- feeling that nothing can go wrong
- outbursts of anger
- alcohol and drug abuse
- increased sexual activity

As Kay Redfield Jamison, a psychologist diagnosed with manic depression, writes in her memoir *An Unquiet Mind:*

> When you're high it's tremendous. The ideas and feelings are fast and frequent like shooting stars and you follow them until you find better and brighter ones. Shyness goes. The right words and gestures are suddenly there, the power to captivate others is a felt certainty. Feelings of ease, intensity, power, well-being, financial omnipotence and euphoria pervade one's marrow.

On hearing this description of mania, people often respond, "If this is a disease, where do I sign up for it?" The problem with mania, however, is that due to the impulsivity and poor judgment that it brings, an episode can wreak havoc on family, friends, the community, and the law. Moreover, when the high inevitably wears off, the individual comes crashing down into a state of total darkness and despair. As Jamison describes:

> A floridly psychotic mania was followed, inevitably, by a long and lacerating black, suicidal depression.

Everything—every thought, word and movement—
was an effort. Everything that once was sparkling now
was flat. I seemed to myself to be dull, boring, inade-
quate, thick brained, unlit, unresponsive, chill skinned,
bloodless, and sparrow drab. I doubted, completely,
my ability to do anything well. It seemed as though my
mind had slowed down and burned out to the point of
being totally useless.

A well-known myth that perfectly describes the manic
depressive's fall from grace is the myth of Icarus. Icarus, son
of the Greek inventor Daedalus (who built the labyrinth),
received wings of wax from his father. Enamored of his new-
found ability to fly to great heights, Icarus ignored his father's
warning, and in a moment of ecstasy flew too close to the sun.
The heat of the sun melted the wax that held his wings
together, and Icarus crashed into the sea.

The alternation of mania and depression illuminates a second aspect of manic depression—its cyclic nature. Periods of
creativity, productivity, and high energy alternate with times
of fatigue and apparent indifference. Mania leads to depression, which leads to mania, which becomes depression, and so
on. This extreme mood change between peaks and valleys is
dangerous, as shown by the fact that a significant minority of
untreated manic depressives (including many of the artists
listed earlier) commit suicide.

Fortunately, manic depression is highly treatable, due to
the discovery of lithium, a simple salt that in 1949 was acci-
dentally found to have a mood-stabilizing effect on bipolar

individuals. The downside of lithium treatment is that thera-peutic levels of lithium are dangerously close to toxic levels. Lithium poisoning affects the brain and can cause coma and death. Thus, in the initial stages of treatment, a doctor must frequently monitor lithium concentration in the blood. After the lithium blood level stabilizes, you can check levels every six months.

The side effects of lithium can include hand tremors, excessive thirst, excessive urination, weakness, fatigue, memory problems, diarrhea, and possible interference with kidney function. Lithium is often ineffective in treating bipolar patients who are rapid cyclers—those who experience four or more manic-depressive cycles per year. For these and other patients who fail to stabilize on lithium, the drugs Depakote, Tegretol, Topamax, and Neurontin (originally antiseizure medications) are also available.

In addition to taking medication, bipolar individuals can employ a number of preventive strategies to decrease the likelihood of having a full-blown manic attack:

- Recognize the early warning signs of mania—for example, insomnia, surges of energy, making lots of plans, grandiose thinking, speeded-up thinking, over-commitment, excessive euphoria, spending too much money, and so on. Let friends and family know of these symptoms so they can also become alerted to the start of a manic episode. Once you become aware of your early symptoms, you can take steps to stabilize yourself.

- Create a stable lifestyle in which you keep regular sleep hours. Studies show that intervals between manic episodes are considerably longer in those people who live in stable environments. In addition, eat a diet that is high in complex carbohydrates and protein, avoiding foods such as simple sugars that can cause ups and downs in some people. You should also avoid alcohol and caffeine in excess.

- Use planning and scheduling to stay focused and grounded. Make a list of things to do and stick to it.

- Try to engage in a daily meditative activity that focuses and calms the mind. If you are too restless for sitting meditation, go for a leisurely walk, taking long, deep breaths along the way.

- Refrain from taking on too many projects or becoming overstimulated. If you feel an excess of energy starting to overtake you, channel it into productive physical activities such as doing the dishes, mopping the floor, cleaning out the basement, weeding a garden, and so on. If these activities begin to disrupt your normal routines, you may be entering a manic cycle. Call your doctor.

- Psychotherapy and support groups can help you explore the emotional aspects of the illness as well as provide support during times of stress.

- If you feel that things are getting out of hand, call your doctor or therapist. This is especially true if you start losing sleep, as sleep deprivation is one of the major contributors to mania.

- Ask a good friend or family member to track your activity level. Share with this person your early warning signs of mania. Sometimes a manic episode can "sneak up on you," and an objective person may spot it before it gets out of hand and guide you to take appropriate action.

Dysthymia

"Good morning, Eeyore," said Pooh.

"Good morning, Pooh Bear," said Eeyore gloomily. "If it is a good morning," he said. "Which I doubt." said he.

—A. A. Milne, *The House at Pooh Corner*

In addition to major depression, another type of depressive illness exists—*dysthymia*—that is far less severe, though crippling in its own way. Dysthymia consists of long-term chronic symptoms that do not disable, but keep one from feeling really good or from functioning at full steam. Physically, it is akin to having a chronic low-grade infection—you never develop a full-blown illness, but always feel a little run-down.

Although dysthymia implies having an inborn tendency to experience a depressed mood, childhood trauma, adjustment problems during adolescence, difficult life transitions, the trauma of personal losses, unresolved life problems, and chronic stress may also cause it. Any combination of these factors can lead to an enduring case of the blues.

Some of the most prominent symptoms of dysthymia are as follows:

- depressed mood for most of the day, for more days than not, for at least two years
- difficulty sleeping
- difficulty in experiencing pleasure
- a hopeless or pessimistic outlook
- low energy or fatigue
- low self-esteem
- difficulty in concentrating or making decisions
- persistent physical symptoms (such as headaches, digestive disorders, or chronic pain) that do not respond to treatment

A dysthymic disorder is characterized not by episodes of illness but by the steady presence of symptoms (see diagram on the opposite page. Because dysthymia does not incapacitate like major depression, as a rule, dysthymic people do well in psychotherapy (you can also use medication). During stressful times, a person with dysthymia may be catapulted into a major depressive episode, called "double depression."

Dysthymic disorder is a common ailment, affecting about 3 to 5 percent of the general population. Unfortunately, because dysthymia is not as severe as clinical depression, the condition is often undiagnosed or dismissed as a case of psychosomatic illness. ("Your symptoms are all in your head," is the all-too-common response from doctors.) Perhaps the most famous dysthymic is Eeyore, the despondent and downcast donkey in A. A. Milne's *Winnie the Pooh*. If you identify with Eeyore (or feel down in the dumps most of the time), it is important that you consult a qualified mental health professional who can make a correct diagnosis.

Having a dysthymic temperament also brings with it positive traits. Dysthymic individuals can be serious, profound, deep, prudent, dependable, industrious, patient, and responsible.

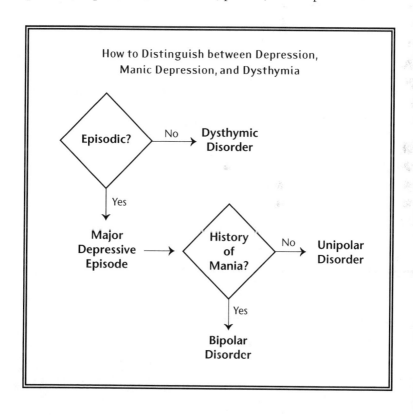

How to Distinguish between Depression, Manic Depression, and Dysthymia

Cyclothymia

Cyclothymia is a milder form of manic depression, character-ized by *hypomania* (a mild form of mania) alternating with mild bouts of depression. The symptoms are similar to those of bipolar illness but less severe. Many cyclothymic disorder patients have difficulty succeeding in their work or social lives because their unpredictable moods and irritability create a great deal of stress, making it difficult to maintain stable per-sonal or professional relationships.

Cyclothymic persons may have a history of multiple geo-graphic moves and alcohol or substance abuse. Nevertheless, when they focus their creative energy toward a worthwhile goal, they may become high achievers in art, business, govern-ment, and so on. (The cycles of cyclothymia are far shorter than in manic depression.) The ability to work long hours with a minimum of sleep when they are hypomanic (mildly manic) often leads to periods of great productivity.

If you identify with the diagnosis of cyclothymia, you may use the wellness strategies described for manic depression, as well as those found this book that elevate and stabilize your mood. If your highs and lows begin to intensify, seek treat-ment with a psychiatrist or mental health professional.

Postpartum Depression

In the period that follows giving birth to a child, many women experience some type of emotional disturbance or mental dysfunction. These "baby blues" are characterized by grief, tearfulness, irritability, and clinging dependence. Such feelings, which may last several days, have been ascribed to the woman's rapid change in hormone levels, the stress of childbirth, and the awareness of the increased responsibility that motherhood brings.

In some cases, however, the baby blues may take on a life of their own, lasting weeks, months, and even years. When this occurs, the woman suffers from *postpartum depression*—a syndrome very much like a major depressive disorder. Anxiety and panic may also accompany this depression. In extreme cases, symptoms may include psychotic features and delusions, especially concerning the newborn infant. Suicidal ideation and obsessive thoughts of violence to the child may exist.

It is estimated that approximately four hundred thousand women in the United States experience postpartum depression, usually six to eight weeks after giving birth. Postpartum depression is a treatable illness that responds to the following modalities:

- recognizing and accepting the disorder
- breaking negative thought patterns
- creating support systems
- reducing stressors in one's life
- exercise and right diet
- medication (antidepressants and antianxiety drugs)
- psychotherapy

A good introduction to this often undiagnosed disorder is contained in the book *This Isn't What I Expected* by Karen

Kleiman, M.S.W., and Valerie Raskin, M.D. You might also want to visit the Web site of the organization Depression after Delivery (www.behavenet.com/dadinc).

Seasonal Affective Disorder

There's a certain Slant of light,

Winter Afternoons—

That oppresses, like the Heft

Of Cathedral Tunes—

Heavenly Hurt, it gives us.

–Emily Dickinson

People with seasonal affective disorder (SAD) tend to experience depressive symptoms during a particular time of the year, most commonly fall or winter. The symptoms of SAD, also known as "winter depression," often begin in October or November and remit in April or May. The symptoms are listed below:

- altered sleep patterns, with overall increased amount of sleep
- difficulty in getting out of bed in the morning and starting the day
- increased lethargy and fatigue
- apathy, sadness, and/or irritability
- increased appetite, carbohydrate craving, and weight gain
- decreased physical activity

Researchers believe that winter's reduction in daylight hours, which desynchronizes the body clock and disturbs the circadian rhythms, causes seasonal affective disorder. Winter depression is usually treated by morning exposure to bright artificial light. By providing appropriately timed light exposure, the body's circadian rhythms become resynchronized, and the symptoms of SAD resolve.

In addition, it is important for the person with SAD to get as much natural light as possible. The following are some suggestions:

- Light up your homes as much as you need to. Use white wallpaper and light-colored carpet instead of dark paneling and dark carpet.
- Choose to live in dwellings with large windows.
- Allow light to shine through doors and windows when temperatures are moderate. Trim hedges around windows to let in more light.
- Exercise outdoors.
- Set up reading or work spaces near a window.
- Ask to sit near a window in restaurants, classrooms, or at your workplace.
- Arrange a winter vacation in a warm, sunny climate.
- Put off large undertakings until the summer.

Although the most common form of recurrent seasonal depressions in northern countries is the winter SAD, researchers at the National Institute of Mental Health uncovered a type of summer depression that occurs during June,

July, and August. Summer SAD tends to occur more in the southern states such as Florida, as well as in Japan and China. Summer depressives frequently ascribe their symptoms to the severe heat of summer, although in some instances intense light may trigger the depressions.

For further information or support about SAD, contact your doctor or visit the Web site of the Society for Light Treatment and Biological Rhythms (www.websciences.org/sltbr). Norman Rosenthal's seminal book *Winter Blues* is also a good resource.

Generalized Anxiety Disorder

There may be no rest for the wicked, but compared to the rest that anxious people get, the wicked undoubtedly have a pastoral life.

—Russell Hampton, *The Far Side of Despair*

Although no one knows exactly why, anxiety accompanies a great number of depressions. In one study, 85 percent of those with major depression were also diagnosed with generalized anxiety disorder (see the symptoms listed on the opposite page), while 35 percent had symptoms of a panic disorder. Because they so often go hand in hand, anxiety and depression are considered the fraternal twins of mood disorders. Believed to be caused in part by a malfunction of brain chemistry, generalized anxiety is not the normal apprehension that one feels before taking a test or awaiting the outcome of a biopsy. A person with an anxiety disorder suffers from what President Franklin Roosevelt called "fear itself." For a reason that is only partially known, the brain's fight-or-flight mechanism becomes activated, even when no real threat exists. Being chronically anxious is like being stalked by an imaginary tiger. The feeling of being in danger never goes away.

How do you know if you suffer from clinical anxiety? The following criteria come from the *Diagnostic and Statistical Manual of Mental Disorders* (DSM-IV). If you or someone you know experiences these symptoms, seek professional assistance.

- Excessive anxiety and worry occur more days than not for at least six months.
- You find it difficult to control the worry and anxiety.
- The anxiety and worry are associated with three (or more) of the following six symptoms:

  1. Restlessness or feeling keyed up or on edge
  2. Being easily fatigued
  3. Difficulty concentrating or mind going blank
  4. Irritability
  5. Muscle tension
  6. Sleep disturbances (difficulty falling or staying asleep, or restless, unsatisfying sleep)

- The anxiety, worry, or physical symptoms cause clinically significant distress or impairment in social, occupational, or other important areas of functioning.
- The disturbance is not due to the direct physiological effects of a substance (for example, drug abuse or a medication) or a general medical condition (for example, hyperthyroidism).

As we shared on Day 21, the best way to treat generalized anxiety disorder is through a combination of diet, exercise, deep breathing, cognitive therapy, and medication.

Panic Disorder

A panic disorder is a specific kind of anxiety disorder that takes a feeling of unease and explodes it into a full-blown panic attack. Imagine you are sitting, comfortably reading a book, and suddenly a feeling of dread overcomes you. Your heart begins to race so much you think you are having a heart attack. You start to sweat and have difficulty catching your breath. You feel terrified as you move around in a vain attempt to get more oxygen. Then, as unexpectedly as they appear, these symptoms end within a few hours.

According to the DSM-IV, four or more of the following symptoms must develop abruptly and come to a peak within ten minutes to diagnose you with a panic disorder:

- palpitations, pounding heart, or accelerated heart rates
- sweating
- trembling or shaking
- sensations of shortness of breath or smothering
- feeling of choking
- chest pain or discomfort
- nausea or abdominal distress
- feeling dizzy, unsteady, lightheaded, or faint
- feelings of unreality or being detached from oneself
- fear of losing control or going crazy

- fear of dying
- numbness or tingling sensations
- chills or hot flashes

Like generalized anxiety, panic attacks result from a malfunction of your body's inborn "fight-or-flight" response that is meant to keep us safe when we sense extreme danger. Many researchers believe panic attacks occur in people whose neurochemical threshold for activating the fight-or-flight response is so low that the most minute environmental or psychological stressors trigger it. Others propose that primarily psychological factors cause panic attacks. For example, some people who have been previously traumatized become "hypervigilant" about any unusual body sensations, quickly reacting to them with extreme fear and creating bodily symptoms that lead to a full-blown panic.

These two theories result in the two ways that clinicians treat panic disorder—physiologically and psychologically. The physiological component of panic disorder is treated with exercise, deep breathing, diet, massage, chiropractic, acupuncture, and medications that help calm the nervous system. The medications include antidepressants such as Paxil, which treats the anxiety that often is a side effect of depression. Antianxiety medications such as Xanax, Ativan, and Klonopin block the symptoms of panic more quickly—in a few days—but are also addictive and often require high doses to be effective.

Psychologically, cognitive-behavioral therapy can teach you how to prevent uncomfortable sensations from escalating into a panic attack. You can learn that it is normal to experience a wide variety of body sensations. Thus, if you feel a palpitation of the heart or shallowness in the breath, give yourself suggestions such as "I am okay. These sensations will pass momentarily" or "I am taking some long, deep breaths until these sensations subside."

Agoraphobia

The term *agoraphobia* is derived from the Greek roots meaning "fear of the marketplace." Panic disorders often lead to agoraphobia in the following way: Let's say your first panic attack occurs while shopping in a grocery store. The next time you go grocery shopping, you begin to anticipate that something in the store—such as the crowds of people—will set off another attack. This hypersensitivity may in fact bring on more panic. Now you have conditioned yourself to associate going to the store with having a panic attack, so you avoid the store entirely.

With agoraphobia, the feared situations can include being in a crowd, standing in a line, being on a bridge, traveling in a bus, train, or automobile, or simply leaving the home. Some people become prisoners of their own homes. Others can enter into a clearly defined "safe zone" (such as walking to the neighborhood grocery store), but become very anxious when venturing into the rest of the world. Bringing along a trusted friend or companion may make it easier to venture out.

As with panic disorder and generalized anxiety disorder, medication and psychotherapy are the two modalities clinicians use to treat agoraphobia. In addition, I have seen ECT (electroconvulsive therapy) work with an older client who suffered from agoraphobia and panic disorder.

Other treatments for agoraphobia include *in vivo desensitization*, in which you guide the person in gradually encountering the situations they find fearful. You can also guide them in coping techniques, such as breathing along with their fearful body sensations rather than trying to fight the sensations or control them.

One key to agoraphobia is to remember that the person is not really afraid of the situation (although they feel like they are), but rather are afraid of their body sensations provoked by the situation. This is called "fear of fear." They feel the beginning of fear and then catastrophize that it will turn into some worse fear, such as fainting, making a fool of themselves, or going crazy. Instead of trying to control the feeling, they need to "go with" the feeling and stay in the present. For example, they might say, "'I feel bad, but I'm living through this moment. I feel terrible, but in this moment, I'm not fainting or going crazy," and so on.

Finally, many times agoraphobics don't have solid, supportive relationships in their lives. They need to form relationships with people with whom they can be assertive and who are responsive to them. Many agoraphobics are non-assertive, making them feel powerlesss and out of control in their lives.

Social Phobia (Social Anxiety Disorder)

Social phobia comes about when a person fears performance in specific types of interpersonal activities or social situations. The individual fears that he or she will act in a humiliating or embarrassing way. Exposure to the feared social situation invariably provokes anxiety, which may cause blushing, trembling, sweating, locking up with fear, or a full-blown panic attack. The most common fear of this type is the fear of public speaking. Other performance fears include fears of using a public restroom while others are present, playing a musical instrument in concert, singing in front of people, or eating in a restaurant.

As a result of these fears, the person avoids the anxiety-provoking social situation. This may interfere with the person's normal routine and cause significant impairment of occupational function, social activities, or relationships.

Treatment for social phobia often includes replacing the terrible things people say to themselves with positive self-talk. The client also needs help learning basic conversational skills, such as how to open and close a conversation. One nice idea is that "an interested person is interesting." If you're interested in what the other person says, that helps, and if you have interests in your life, that helps too. Social phobics should have help practicing in situations of graded difficulty so they gradually expose themselves to fearful situations.

Post-Traumatic Stress Disorder

The syndrome we call post-traumatic stress disorder (PTSD) was first observed on the battlefield and was known as "shell shock" or "battle fatigue." It wasn't until the Vietnam War, however, that the malady was formally diagnosed as a psychiatric condition.

The essence of PTSD is that after a traumatic event, the individual continually relives the event in different ways, such as through flashbacks and nightmares, and continues to feel helpless and terrified. Of course, horrifying events are by no means restricted to war victims. Natural disasters such as earthquakes, floods, tornadoes, and fires strike many communities. Other traumas include car accidents, industrial accidents, torture, rape, physical and sexual abuse, abandonment, neglect, and growing up in an alcoholic family.

The following are the symptoms of PTSD as listed in the DSM-IV:

- The person has been exposed to a traumatic event in which both of the following were present:

  1. The person experienced, witnessed, or was confronted with an event or events that involved actual or threatened death or serious injury or a threat to the physical integrity of self or others.
  2. The person's response involved intense fear, helplessness, or horror.

- The traumatic event persists in one of the following ways:

  1. Recurrent and intrusive distressing recollections of the event
  2. Nightmares
  3. Acting or feeling as if the event is recurring
  4. Avoiding things that are associated with the traumatic event
  5. Feeling detached from life
  6. Never expecting to have a normal life
  7. Difficulty falling or staying asleep
  8. Irritability or outbursts of anger
  9. Difficulty concentrating
  10. Hypervigilance
  11. Exaggerated startle response

- These symptoms occur for more than one month and cause problems with work, relationships, and other important areas of functioning.

The symptoms of PTSD respond to a combination of both medication and psychotherapy. The central aspect of psychotherapy is catharsis, the reexperiencing and expressing of the feelings one had at the time of the trauma. Although it may seem like a good idea to try to avoid or forget about the painful memories, when repressed, they tend to resurface in the form of nightmares or fearful images and flashbacks. However, when you face your fears instead of avoiding them, they have less control over you.

One way to face one's fears is through exposure therapy, which allows the individual to come in contact with the triggers that evoke the traumatic event (for example, the scene of the crime, the site of the accident, the field of combat). You can combine this with other techniques of anxiety reduction such as deep muscle relaxation, biofeedback, or diaphragmatic breathing.

Medication is another useful tool in overcoming PTSD. Because depression often accompanies PTSD, antidepressants are usually the first choice of medication. Antianxiety drugs are used to deal with arousal and insomnia, but because many people with PTSD are prone to substance abuse, use these with caution.

Finally, a recently developed therapy called Eye Movement Desensitization Reprocessing (EMDR) offers great promise in helping people release the symptoms of trauma. EMDR therapy uses rapid eye movement, which activates opposite sides of the brain, releasing emotional experiences that are "trapped" in the nervous system. This assists the nervous system to free itself of blockages and restructure itself. Once you release the stress surrounding the traumatic event, the emotionally difficult memories also subside. To learn more about EMDR, visit the Web site www.emdr.com.

Alcohol and Substance Abuse Disorders

Substance abuse is a huge problem in the United States. Aside from creating suffering in the user, substance abuse contributes to car and work accidents, divorce, crime, violence, suicide, lost productivity, and social chaos. A plethora of substances can cross the blood-brain barrier to influence mood and behavior. The DMS-IV divides the most widely used of these substances into eleven specific categories: alcohol, amphetamines, caffeine, cannabis, cocaine, hallucinogens, inhalants, nicotine, opioids, phencyclidine, sedatives, and another miscellaneous category of less commonly abused substances.

Many people report that they turn to drugs and alcohol to medicate intense psychological or emotional pain. Those who do so add chemical dependency to the problem of a mood disorder and thus have a "dual diagnosis." Once a person with dual diagnosis becomes clean and sober, he or she must still deal with the original source of the pain—the mental/emotional disorder. It is my hope that through this book and the many other wonderful resources that exist in the field of mental health, increasing numbers of people will heal from their emotional pain, thereby lessening the chance of becoming trapped in addiction.

Appendix B

Sample Affirmations
for Everyday Use

❧

To assist you in applying affirmations to your daily life, a series of sample affirmations are listed under six distinct headings: Self-Love/Self-Esteem, Love and Relationships, Health and Healing, Work/Vocation, Prosperity, and Spiritual Development.

Use these categories to work with specific goals or challenges in your life. Thus, if your work and career are a major focus right now, turn to the Work/Vocation list of affirmations. After reading them over, you could choose from the ones listed or use them as a launching point to create your own. Allow yourself to be drawn to those affirmations that have the most significance for you.

I use the words "God," "higher power," "spirit," "divine intelligence," "the universe," and so on in many of the affirmations that follow. The use of such terms reflects my own spiritual orientation toward life. If these concepts feel foreign or uncomfortable to you, feel free to substitute a more secular language.

Affirmations for Self-Love/Self-Esteem

I like myself.

I value myself.

I have something unique to offer.

I deserve to be happy.

I treat myself to the very best.

I am a good person.

I love myself just the way I am.

I accept myself as I am.

I feel good about me.

I like my essence.

I take responsibility for my well-being.

I take good care of myself.

I respect who I am.

I am pure spirit, forever connecting with the wonderful presence of love.

I am the writer, director, and actor of my own movie. I like what I see.

I am confident and self-assured.

I trust myself.

I am the master of my fate. I am the captain of my soul.

Affirmations for Love and Relationships

I have love to share.

I am learning to love myself.

Love flows to and from me.

I radiate love to everyone I encounter.

I am lovable.

I am a magnet for open, loving relationships. I draw to myself my ideal partner and friends. I radiate love to everyone, and I am loved in return.

I feel good about being close.

I enjoy expressing my sexuality.

I am willing to risk myself in love.

I deserve love.

I am clear about what I want in a relationship.

I am ready for a relationship. I am ready for love.

I cherish the male and female aspects of myself.

I deserve to be with a partner who loves me.

I deserve to have a fulfilling and functional relationship.

As a result of my inner healing work, I attract loving energy in a primary relationship.

I am attracting a partner who loves him-/herself as much as I love myself.

I am attracting a partner who loves me as much as I love him/her.

I now attract a loving, intimate, fun, joyful relationship with my lifetime partner with whom I will raise a family.

The presence of God acts in perfect ways to guide me to my highest good in my relationships. I willingly release any thought of separation.

Affirmations for Health and Healing

I feel vital and alive.

Every day in every way, I am getting better and better.

I treat my body like royalty.

I love my body.

My body is the perfect size and shape.

My body is strong and flexible.

The perfection of my divine being daily bathes all the cells of my body.

I open my mind and heart to the healing love of God. Every organ, cell, and tissue is bathed in the revitalizing light of Spirit.

I am healthy, happy, and radiant.

I radiate good health.

My body is a safe and pleasurable place for me to be.

My sleep is relaxed and refreshing.

I have all the energy I need to accomplish my goals.

God's love heals me and makes me whole.

The healing power of God within is a limitless wellspring of life, strength, and vitality.

I turn my thoughts to God each day and visualize vibrant health in every cell. I trust that healing is taking place.

My body fairly sizzles with vitality and wholeness. I am invigorated each and every day as I contemplate the perfection of Spirit within me and its amazing power to heal.

My body is healed, restored, and filled with energy.

Affirmations for Work/Vocation

I am at the center of the divine idea of my right and perfect work for creative fulfillment, service to God, and financial abundance.

I am economically grounded, financially self-sufficient, and happy in my work through the heartfelt expression of my creative and mental skills.

I attract the people, circumstances, and finances to make my business succeed.

By doing what I love, I make a comfortable living.

I have clarity about what I want to do for a living.

I freely give of my talents, doing what I love, and I am divinely compensated.

I have found a fulfilling career to support myself in the world.

I am financially self-sufficient and happy in my work.

I have wonderful work in a wonderful way.

I give wonderful service for wonderful pay.

God is my silent partner in my work.

Creative and practical ideas inspire me each and every day.

God is guiding me to fulfilling work.

I am actualizing my full potential in the world.

My work is love in action.

My career is moving onward and upward.

I have positive relationships with my coworkers (or boss, employees, business partners, and so on).

I feel great about what I do for a living.

I acknowledge and honor myself for my contributions at work.

Through my work, I share my gifts and talents.

My creativity finds expression in my work.

I bring passion to my work.

Affirmations for Prosperity

I deserve to be prosperous.

God is my source. I release my worry and anxiety about money.

I have all the time, money, and energy I need to do what is most important to me.

I release my fear of lack and replace it with my faith in my abundant supply.

Success and prosperity continue to flow into and bless my life.

Money flows freely into my life. I use it for my good.

Divine love always has and divine love always will supply my every need.

Divine intelligence now inspires me with prosperous ideas.

Money is always available for good ideas.

I am abundantly compensated for my creative ideas.

I love what I do, and that love brings me the money I need.

All financial doors are open. All financial channels are free. The right amount of money now comes to me.

I live in an abundant universe.

The inexhaustible supply of spirit is equal to every demand. There is no reality in lack. Abundance is here and now manifest.

My financial worth increases every day.

Every dollar I circulate enriches the economy and comes back to me multiplied.

All of my investments are profitable, either monetarily or in valuable experience.

I have the ability to create financial support for myself in my life.

I lift up my heart and mind to the awareness that God in me is my unlimited, overflowing supply of every kind of good.

The goodness of God is my source. I give thanks for the ever-increasing abundance that flows freely to me and from me to bless others.

I always have enough money.

Money is a renewable resource.

I have more than I need, and so I share with the world.

My cup runneth over.

More than enough exists to go around for everyone, including me.

My income exceeds my expenses.

A part of all I earn is mine to keep.

I am financially independent.

I invest wisely and responsibly.

The more I give, the more I am given to give.

My wealth contributes to my good and to the good of others.

I prosper everyone and everyone prospers me.

My personal connection to universal intelligence allows abundance to flow to and through me.

God manifests through my life as abundance and prosperity on all levels.

I rejoice in my continuing good fortune.

I look within for my supply. I keep my eyes on the abundant inner reality, not on outer appearances.

Affirmations for Spiritual Development

The universe nurtures and protects me at all times and in all places.

Everything I need comes to me.

All is well in my life; I am truly blessed.

All things work together for good in my life.

I am a channel for love and healing.

I release my inner barriers to fulfilling my purpose on earth.

I affirm divine order, and all parts of my life fall into place.

God is my instant, constant, and abundant supply of all good.

The presence of God in me is a limitless reservoir of faith, strength, and power. Each day I express more of God's faith and receive more of God's blessings.

God is with me through every change—guiding, protecting, and directing me all the way.

I dwell in the presence of God's eternal love.

The Lord is my shepherd.

I am attuned to divine inspiration.

I constantly communicate with my creative source.

Through God working through me, all things are possible.

I trust my intuition.

As I follow my heart, I am provided for.

When one door closes, another door opens. Whenever I seem to lose something of value, I am open to the possibility that something better may take its place.

I am divinely guided.

Focusing on the present heals my fear of the unknown.

I expect a miracle.

I am worthy to receive the benevolent offerings of the universe.

I see all problems as disguised opportunities.

I listen to intuition and confidently act on what I hear.

I affirm the best for myself and others.

God's wisdom illumines me, casting light on my path.

When I follow my heart, the universe supports me.

I let go and let God.

It's all unfolding perfectly.

Life has great things in store for me.

I give thanks and praise for all things.

This, too, shall pass.

I learn from every situation I encounter.

As I forgive myself and others, I free myself of bondage to the past.

Forgiveness is its own reward.

I bless and release all those who have caused me pain.

As I forgive, so am I forgiven.

My will and the divine will are one.

I am continually aligned with my higher purpose.

Every experience in life brings me closer to God.

My faith makes me whole.

I can change and transform my old and limiting beliefs.

The power to experience miracles is in me now.

I turn my will and my life over to the care of my higher power.

I give thanks for the revelation of the divine plan for my life.

I let go of anything that blocks my experience of good.

I make my spiritual life my highest priority.
I trust in God. I know that God brings me through every
    experience victoriously.
The light of God surrounds me.
The love of God enfolds me.
The power of God protects me.
The presence of God watches over me.
Wherever I am, God is.

Appendix C

How to Create a Vision of Wellness

 ✏

The second habit is this: Begin with the end in mind.

—Steven Covey, *The Seven Habits of Highly Effective People*

On Day 1 of the daily lessons, we stated that setting the intention to heal was the starting point of recovery from any mood disorder. Once you make the decision to get well, you need specific tools to translate your intention to heal into a reality. One such tool is called "a vision statement of wellness." Essentially, your vision statement answers the question, *"What would my life look and feel like if I were free from the symptoms of my emotional disorder?"*

A vision statement is based on the second habit from Steven Covey's *The Seven Habits of Highly Effective People*— "begin with the end in mind." According to Covey, this habit arises from the principle that "all things are created twice"— first in the mind and then in the world of form. In writing a vision statement, you create the exact mental blueprint or picture of health that you seek to bring into your life.

The business community has used vision statements for years. Most organizations have some form of "mission statement" that defines their purpose and informs the way they carry our their daily activities. Olympic athletes also engage in creative visioning through the practice of "visual rehearsal." For example, the gymnast imagines his entire routine before he sets foot on the mat. In so doing, he programs his nervous system to direct his body to perform optimally.

In a similar fashion, you can optimize your body's natural healing system through creating a vision statement of wellness. The following exercise shows you how.

Composing a Vision Statement

Imagine for a moment that you are in a state of health and wholeness. What would it be like for you to be in a better mood?

How would your body look and feel? How much energy would you have?

How would you feel most of the time? What types of thoughts would you think?

What types of relationships would you have? In what kind of work would you be involved? What would your spiritual life be like?

Drawing on the answers to the above questions, write a *paragraph (or more)* describing your vision of mental and emotional health.

See if you can use all five senses—sight, hearing, touch, smell, and taste—to depict your experience. Set it down in the present tense, as if the experience were happening now.

As you proceed with this exercise, do your best to write something, even if recovery from depression seems like a distant reality. If you can't imagine yourself being completely well, choose to see yourself feeling "a little bit better." One woman simply stated, "I just want to feel my life force again." Remember, I am not asking you to believe in your healing, only to desire it.

If this still seems like too much, ask someone to help you write your vision statement, such as a friend, family member, your counselor, and so on. *You don't have to do this work alone.*

On the following pages, I provide three sample vision statements of different lengths and styles. Laura's is short and simple. Barbara's was written by a professional author and is the longest. Michael's is medium length.

Laura's Vision of Health and Wellness

The following vision statement is only two lines, but it perfectly captures the essence of joy and wellness.

I am healed, whole, and complete.
I am fully alive, filled with love, joy, and gratitude.

Barbara's Vision of Health and Wellness

This vision statement was written by Barbara, a professional author and one of the members of my depression support group:

> I am a woman of strength and resilience. I accept the ebb and flow of life with humor and openness, knowing I am always safe. I take Love with me wherever I go. I gratefully receive the love and support of my friends and make my strength, love, and support available to them in appropriate ways.
>
> I can say "no" when I feel overextended and continue to love and accept myself and to be loved and accepted by others. If someone is unused to my saying "no" and becomes upset, I can simply bless them, remembering that they, too, are only human. I continue to love and respect myself.
>
> My body is strong and capable. Every cell hums with vibrant good health. I love to exercise and to feel my body work. I let all body sensations, nervous or otherwise, flow through me as I relax and rest in the comfort and care of a Higher Power. The true me is always at peace.

I enjoy the world and spend time each day in nature and with people. I am eager to start work each day. The work is challenging and fun! I trust my talent and relax into my work schedule, looking forward just as eagerly to the end of the workday—time to venture out into the world!

I love getting out and about, as comfortable when I'm by myself as I am with others. I love to explore new places and new activities. The world seems like a friendly place, and I am secure and strong within it.

I easily stay in touch with friends and family. Whether or not I have accomplished all I expected to, I remember the lilies of the field and the sparrows—they don't work for God's love and care; it is a free gift.

When I get into bed at night, I fall asleep with a peaceful mind, a grateful heart, and a body that feels comfortable and alive. I sleep well and awaken refreshed and with new confidence and energy to begin another adventure!

Michael's Vision of Health and Wellness

Michael, a group member who suffered from anxiety as well as depression, wrote this vision statement to describe his desire to heal.

> I am calm and peaceful. My energy is strong and good. I am engaged in life with my family, friends, and coworkers. I am happy and easygoing. I sleep well and peacefully at night. I wake up in the morning looking forward to my day, whether it is new design challenges at work or weekends when nothing is planned.
>
> I look forward to being with and doing things with my friends and family. I travel extensively and I love it. I am a bodybuilder enjoying my great body and my workouts.
>
> I am a good influence on my kids, and they look to me for advice and support, which I easily and positively give. I love my life.

As these examples illustrate, no specific way exists to compose a vision statement. Your statement doesn't have to be beautifully written—it just needs to speak to you. Trust your own *voice*. Let the words come from your heart. There is no need to compare yourself to others.

Also, don't worry about creating a perfect vision the first time. Over time you can modify your vision if you choose to. My own vision statement went through five drafts until it arrived at its current form.

In addition to putting your vision in writing, you might want to use a visual image or images to depict the state of wellness you seek. For example, meditate on an image, such as a tree, that gives you the feeling of strength and wholeness. Focusing on this image every day will help your subconscious mind make your vision of wellness a reality.

Another option is to create a collage in which you depict images of wellness using cut-out pictures from magazines. When I attended art therapy at day treatment, creating these collages allowed me to give expression to my feelings and dreams that I could not verbalize. A sample of such a collage appears on page 206.

The important thing is to make a start, even if it is to wish for a tiny improvement. Remember, the journey of a thousand miles begins with a single step.

A Picture of Wellness

"A picture is worth a thousand words," says a Chinese proverb. The collage below was created by cutting and pasting images from magazines.* It gives a pictorial representation of someone's vision of wellness.

If you are having a difficult time putting your thoughts and feelings into words, you might consider gathering some old magazines and creating your own wellness collage. Or, if you are artistically inclined, you may want to draw or paint your picture of wellness. The book *Life*, *Paint*, *and Passion* by Michelle Cachou can help you to access important healing images through painting, especially if you have no drawing experience.

About the Author

Douglas Bloch is an author, teacher, and counselor who writes and speaks on the topics of psychology, healing, and spirituality. He earned his B.A. in Psychology from New York University and an M.A. in Counseling from the University of Oregon. He is the author of eleven books, including the best-selling *Words That Heal: Affirmations and Meditations for Daily Living; Healing from Depression; Listening to Your Inner Voice;* and *I Am With You Always*, as well as the parenting book *The Power of Positive Talk.*

Douglas lives in Portland, Oregon, with his partner of twenty years, Joan; their cat, Gabriel; two parakeets, Sebastian and Sebrina; and their turtle, Vishnu. He is available for lectures and workshops. You may contact him at:

Douglas Bloch
4226 NE 23rd Avenue
Portland, OR 97211
503-284-2848; fax 503-284-6754
Email: dbloch@teleport.com
www.healingfromdepression.com

Healing Books by
Douglas Bloch, M.A.

❧

Words That Heal the Blues. A daily mental health recovery program, including affirmations and meditations for living optimally with mood disorders.

Healing From Depression. A comprehensive twelve-week body, mind, and spirit recovery program on healing from depression.

Words That Heal. Both a self-help primer on affirmations and a source of daily inspiration. Contains fifty-two meditations that provide comfort, upliftment, and support. Endorsed by John Bradshaw and Jerry Jampolsky.

Listening to Your Inner Voice. The sequel to Words That Heal. How to discover the truth within you and let it guide your way.

I Am With You Always. A treasury of inspirational quotations, poems, and prayers from history's great spiritual teachers, philosophers, and artists.

The Power of Positive Talk. How to use affirmations to build self-esteem in children. A guide for parents, teachers, and counselors.

To order these books, visit www.healingfromdepression.com

Printed in the United States
by Baker & Taylor Publisher Services